101 THINGS TO DO WITH AN A4 SHEET OF PAPER

ILLUSTRATED BY SARAH DENNIS

EDITED BY JUDITH HANNAM

KYLE BOOKS

First published in Great Britain in 2015 by
Kyle Books, an imprint of Kyle Cathie Ltd.
192–198 Vauxhall Bridge Road
London SW1V 1DX
general.enquiries@kylebooks.com
www.kylebooks.com

10 9 8 7 6 5 4 3 2 1

ISBN 978 0 85783 3334

Editor: Judith Hannam
Designer: Peter Ward
Illustrator: Sarah Dennis
Production: Lisa Pinnell

A Cataloguing in Publication record for this title is available from the British Library.

Printed and bound in Singapore by Tien Wah Press

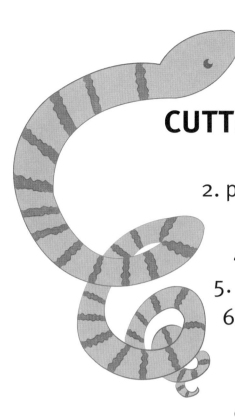

CUTTING & COLOURING

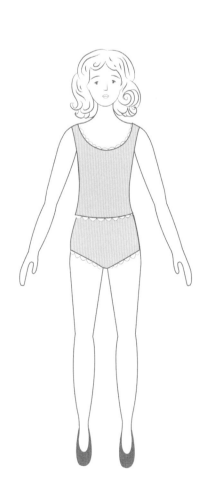

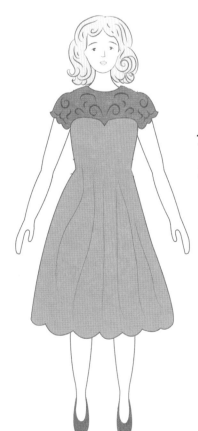

FOLDING

DECORATIONS & FESTIVITIES

MASKS, MOUSTACHES & PARTY HATS

CARDS & ENVELOPES

Page corner bookmark

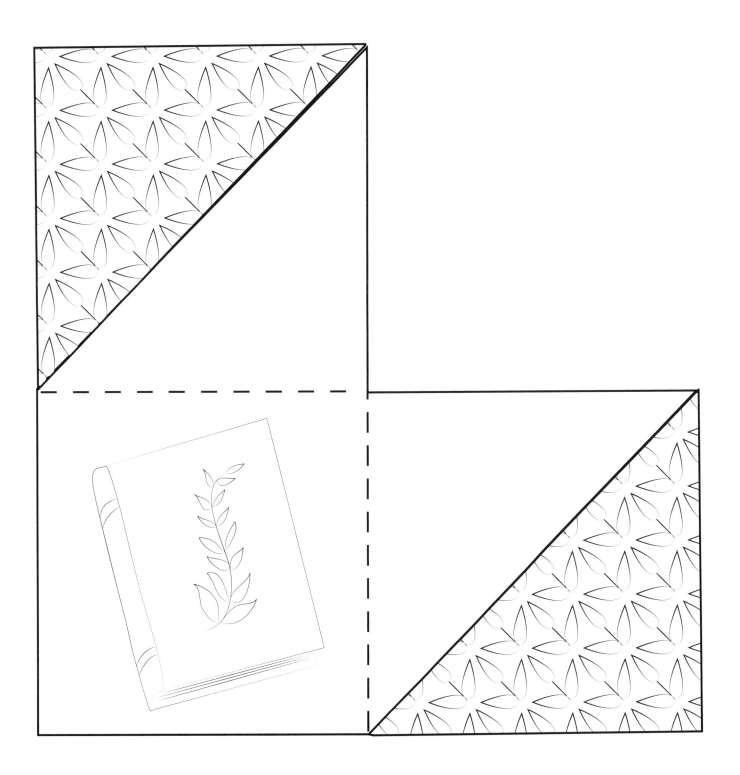

Colour in the template above, cut out and follow the instructions overleaf.

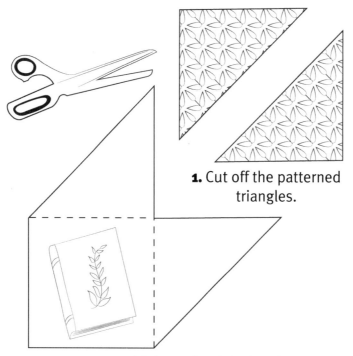

1. Cut off the patterned triangles.

2. Fold down the right-hand corner.

3. Apply glue to the underside of the other corner and stick over the folded down corner. If you want, you can leave your bookmark like this.

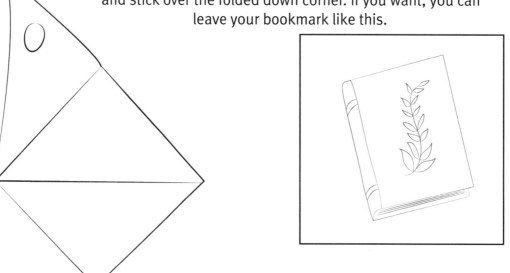

4. Alternatively, glue one of the patterned triangles over the folded down corners and the other to the inside of the bookmark, as shown.

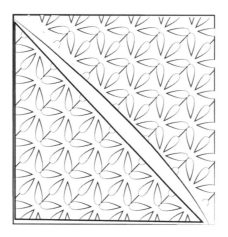

BOOK PLATES

Ex Libris

EX Libris

Paper Chain Doll

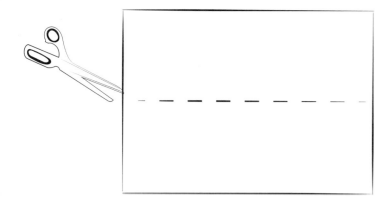

1. Cut your sheet of paper in half lengthways.

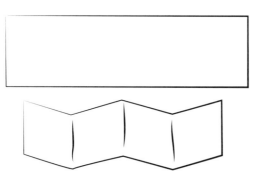

2. Fold each half into quarters, accordion style.

3. Draw your figure on the top layers, making sure that the arms extend beyond the edges.

4. Cut out, unfold and connect the chains using glue or sticky tape.

PAPER CHAIN ANIMALS

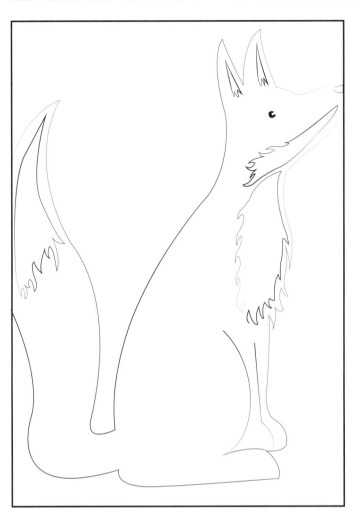

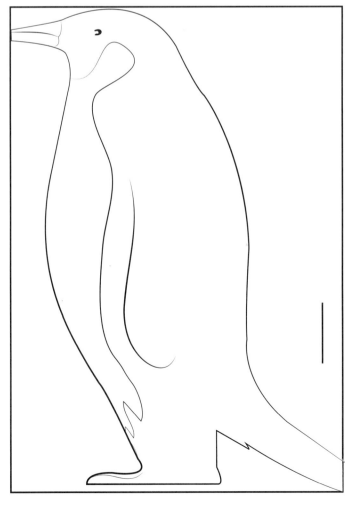

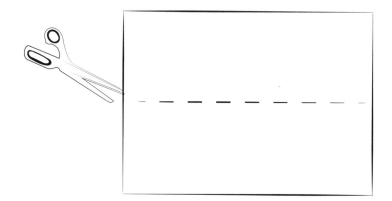

1. Cut your sheet of paper in half lengthways.

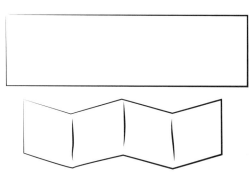

2. Fold each half into quarters, accordion style.

3. Draw your animal on the top layers, making sure that two areas extend beyond the edges.

4. Cut out, unfold and connect the chains using glue or sticky tape.

Paper Chain Snake

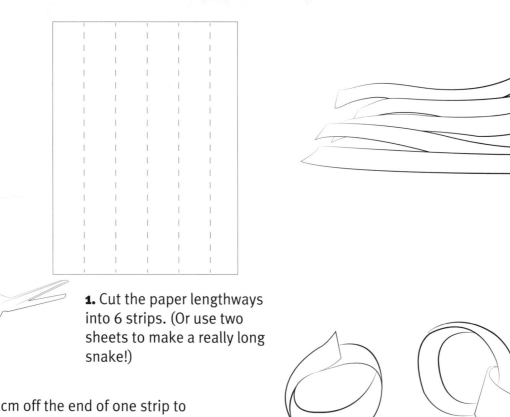

1. Cut the paper lengthways into 6 strips. (Or use two sheets to make a really long snake!)

2. Cut 1cm off the end of one strip to make a tongue.

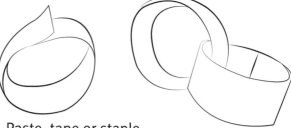

3. Paste, tape or staple the ends of the first strip to form a loop.

4. Link the next strip through the loop and secure as before. Continue until you have the length of snake you want.

5. Decorate with eyes and stick on the tongue.

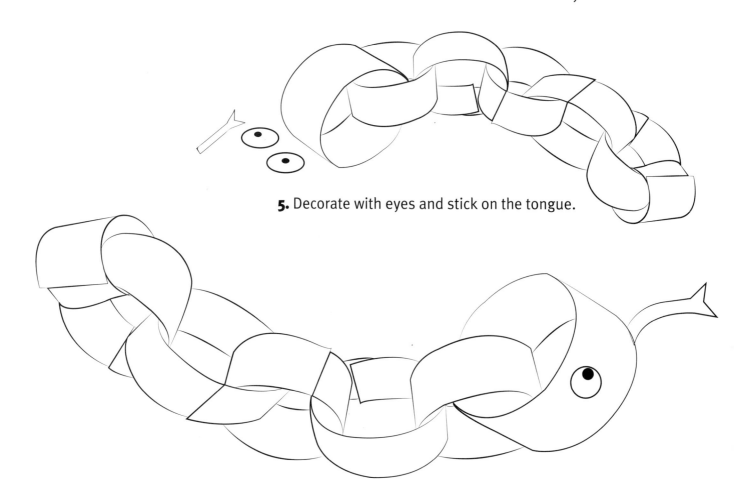

Butterflies

Colour in the templates overleaf, cut out, and either
suspend from thread or use as decorations.

Birds in flight

Colour in the templates overleaf, cut out, and either suspend from thread or use as decorations.

Heart Cake Doily

Cut out the shaded areas using a craft knife.

Cupcake Wrappers

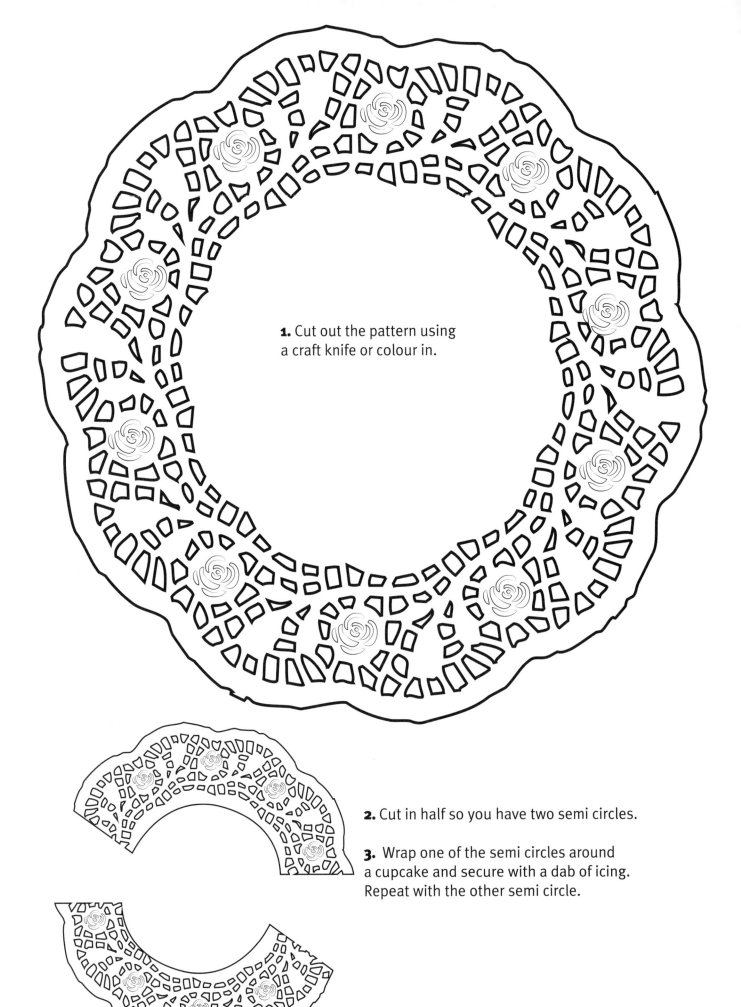

1. Cut out the pattern using a craft knife or colour in.

2. Cut in half so you have two semi circles.

3. Wrap one of the semi circles around a cupcake and secure with a dab of icing. Repeat with the other semi circle.

JOINTED ROBOT PUPPET

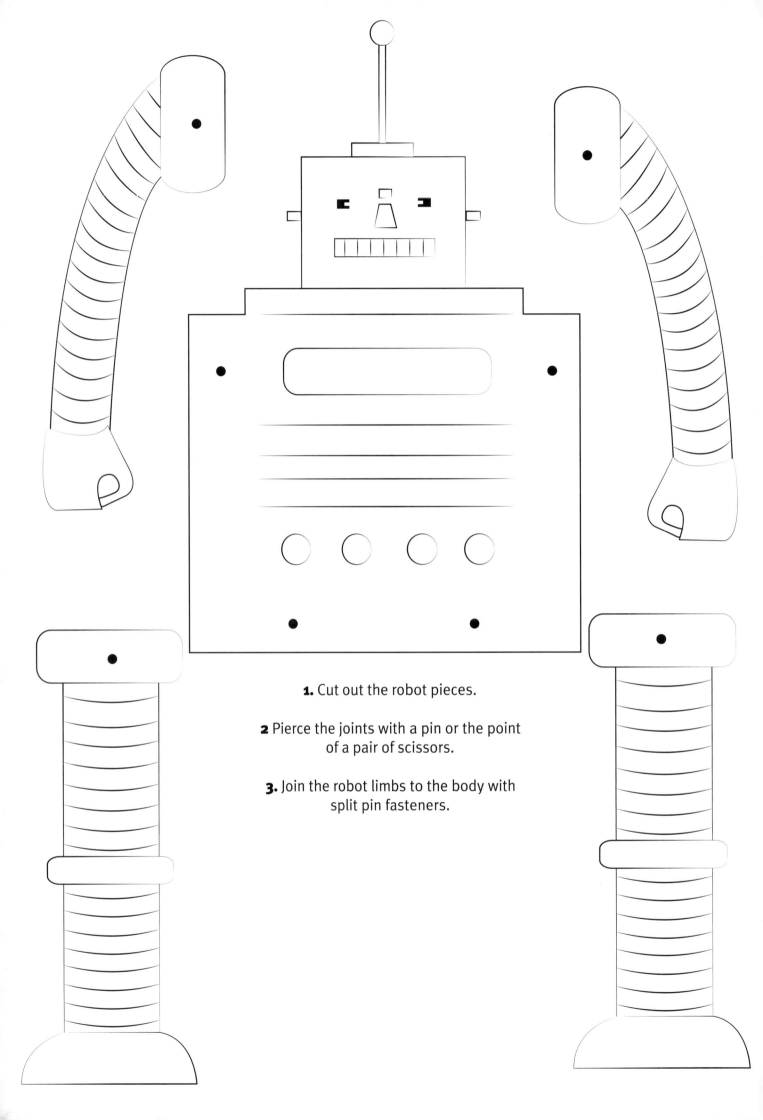

1. Cut out the robot pieces.

2 Pierce the joints with a pin or the point of a pair of scissors.

3. Join the robot limbs to the body with split pin fasteners.

Jointed
Monkey Puppet

1. Cut out the monkey pieces and pierce the joints with a pin or the point of a pair of scissors.

2. Join the monkey's limbs to its body with split pin fastners.

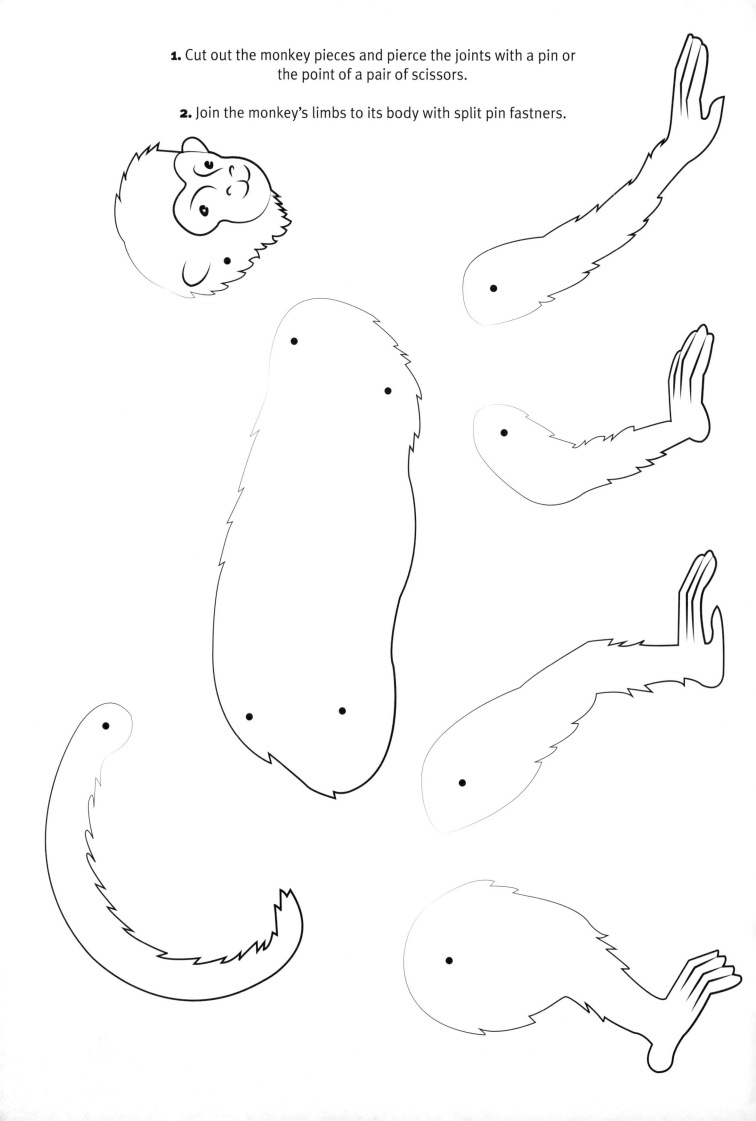

Mermaid Shadow Puppet

1. Cut out the stencil and attach it to a pencil.

2. To create your puppet show, you will need a screen (through which light must be able to pass) on which to project the shadows. This screen can be another sheet of paper. The light (the sun or a lamp) must shine on to the screen. Anything placed between the light source and the screen will cast a shadow.

Hare Shadow Puppets

1. Cut out the stencils and attach them to pencils.

2. To create your puppet show, you will need a screen (through which light must be able to pass) on which to project the shadows. This screen can be another sheet of paper. The light (the sun or a lamp) must shine on to the screen. Anything placed between the light source and the screen will cast a shadow.

Cone Finger Puppet
Cat

1. Colour in your cat.

2. Cut out the body, glue along the length of one edge, and stick the sides together to make a cone that will fit over your finger.

3. Cut out and glue together the front and back parts of the head. Attach to the body. Finally, cut out the tail and stick to the back of the body.

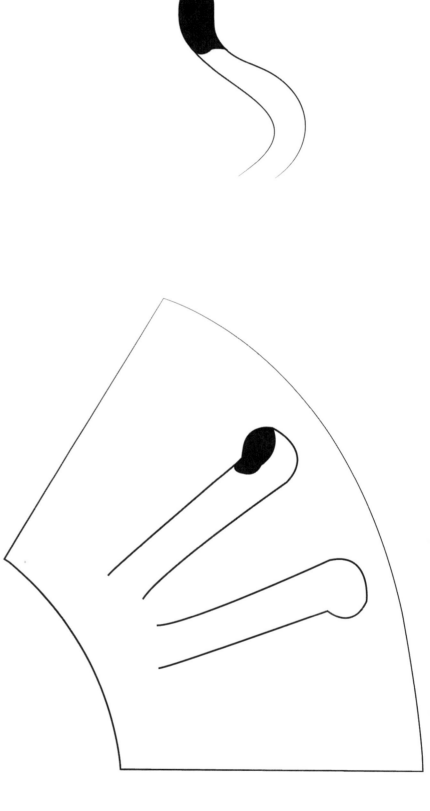

Cone Finger Puppet
Dog

1. Colour in your dog.

2. Cut out the body, glue along the length of one edge, and stick the sides together to make a cone that will fit over your finger.

3. Cut out and glue together the front and back parts of the head. Attach to the body.

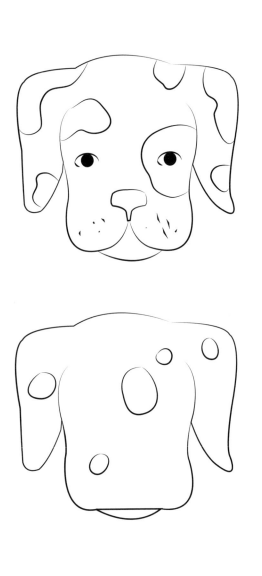

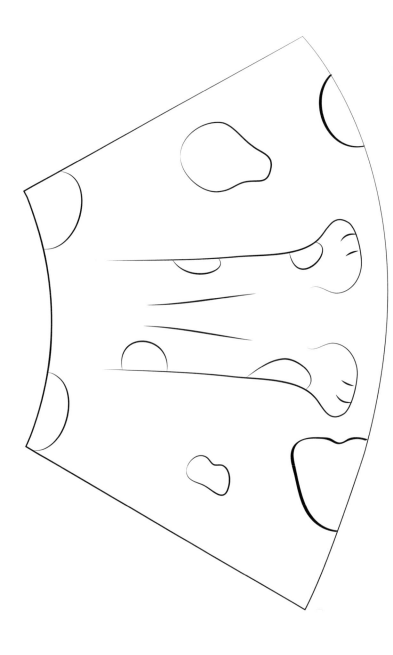

Footballer finger puppets

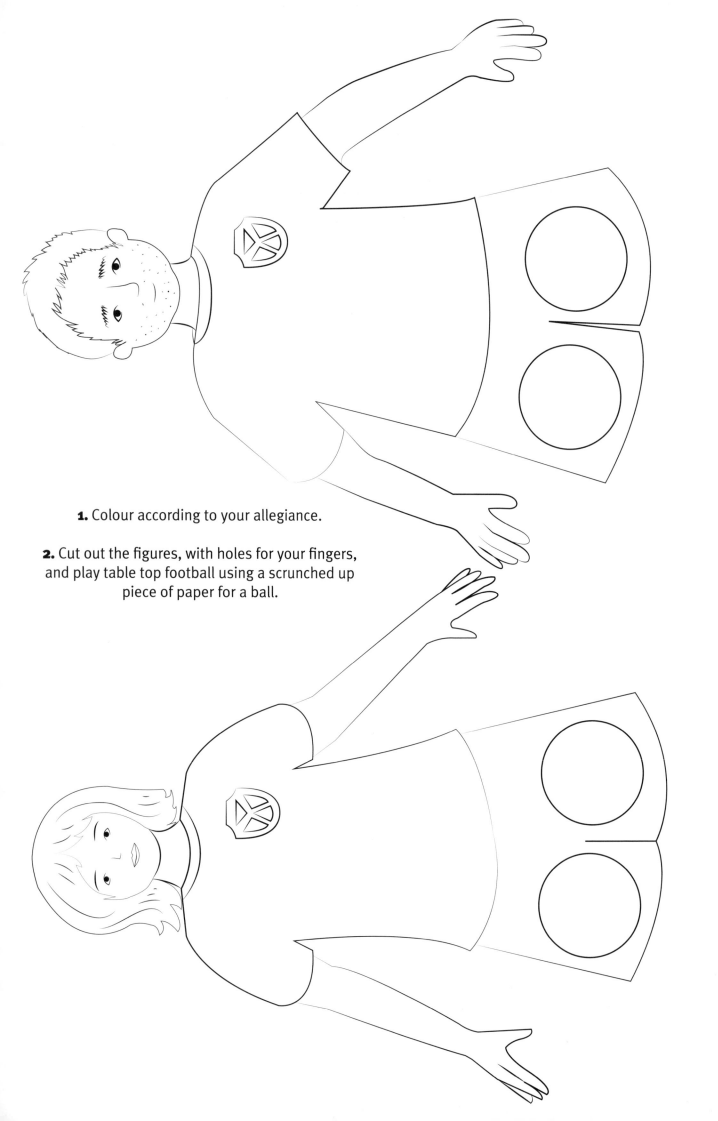

1. Colour according to your allegiance.

2. Cut out the figures, with holes for your fingers, and play table top football using a scrunched up piece of paper for a ball.

Spiral snake

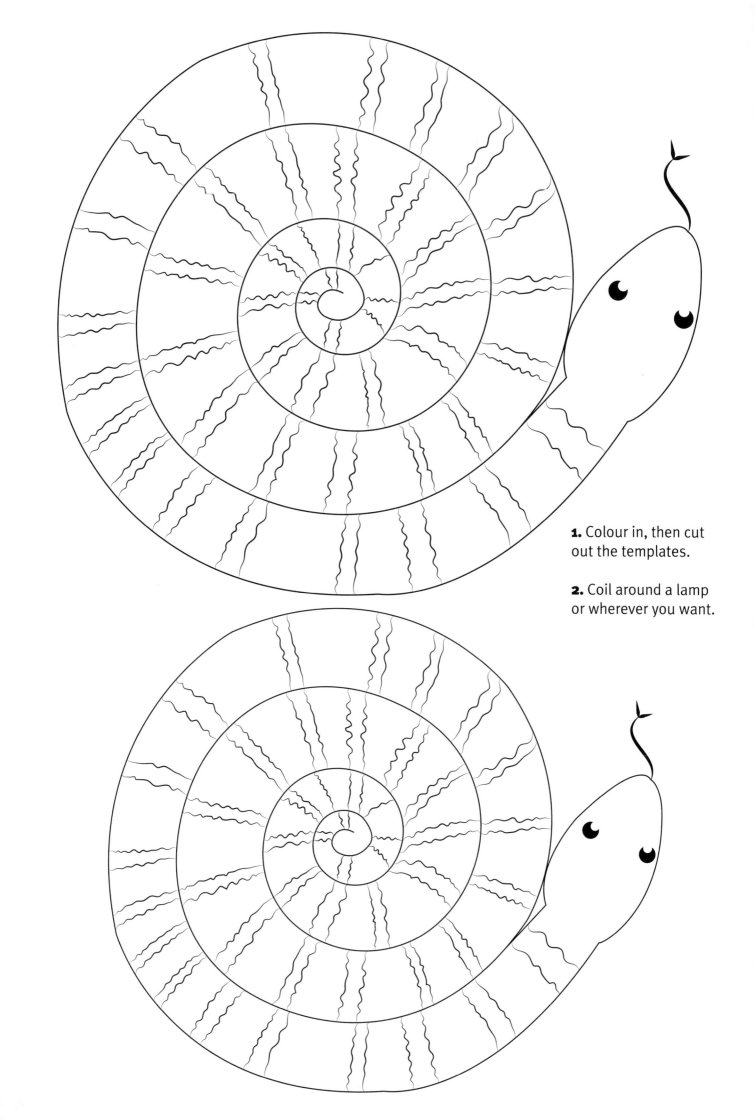

1. Colour in, then cut out the templates.

2. Coil around a lamp or wherever you want.

Three Bears
finger puppets

Colour in, then cut out. Join the ends of the tabs with glue and slip over your fingers.

Dress Your Own Paper Doll

Paper Weaving

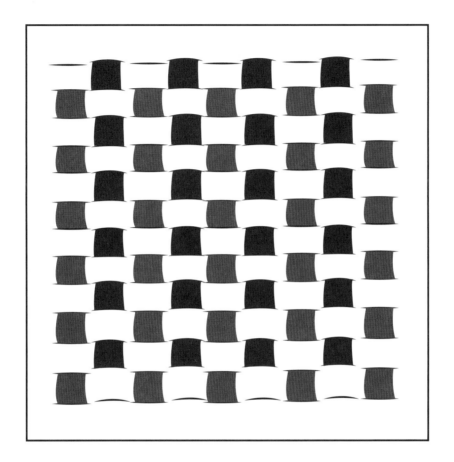

1. Make your sheet of paper into a square by folding the top corner over to form a triangle (do not crease). Cut off the rectangle below the triangle you just formed.

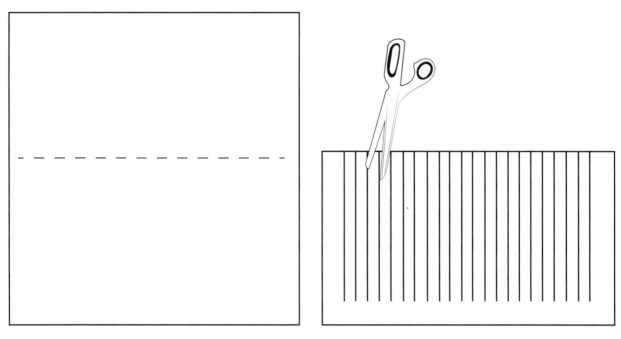

2. Fold the square in half lengthways and cut evenly-spaced slits starting from the folded edge and continuing up to about 1.5cm from the opposite edge.

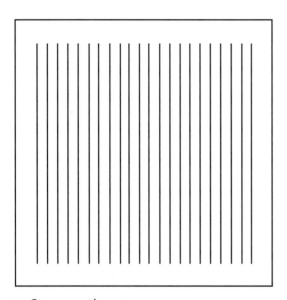

3. Open up the paper.

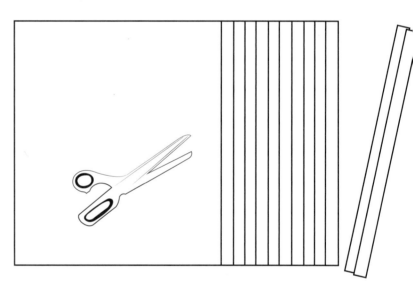

4. Take another sheet of A4 and cut into strips lengthways.

5. Take one of the strips and, beginning from the top, weave over and under the cut slits in the square of paper. Take a second strip and weave in the opposite way – under and over – to the first. Continue until your paper weave is full.

6. Fold the excess lengths of each strip inwards and glue them in place.

NUMERAL STENCIL

1/2/20

1.2.20

Cut out the stencil overleaf and use to
create your own date reminders.

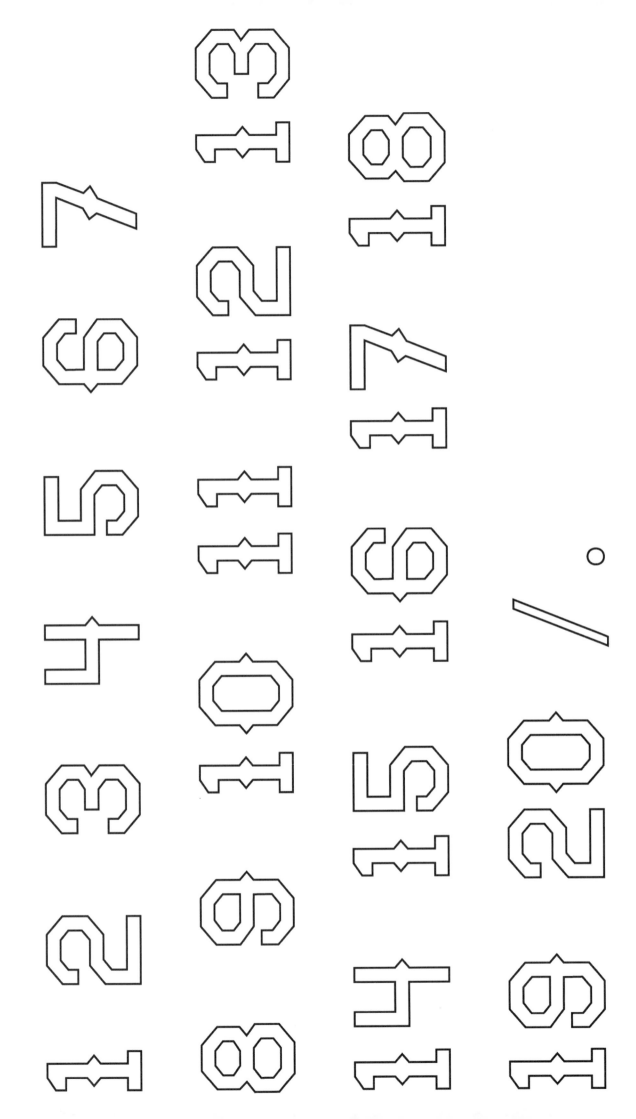

Spider Web

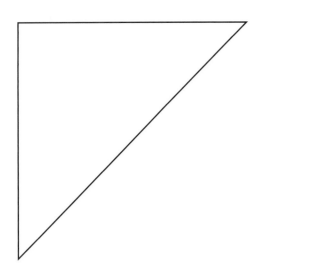

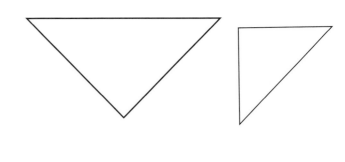

1. Make your sheet of paper into a square by folding the bottom corner over to form a triangle. Cut off the rectangle so that you are left with the folded triangle.

2. Fold the triangle in half by bringing the bottom left-hand corner to meet the top right corner. Fold once more to crate a smaller triangle.

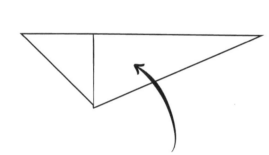

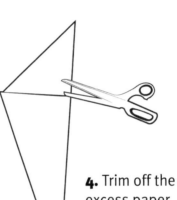

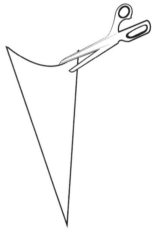

4. Trim off the excess paper, as shown.

3. With the long edge at the top, bring the bottom right-hand side up to meet the long edge, as shown.

5. Cut a curved line across the top corners.

6. Cut out curved rectangles along the folded edge of the paper, almost touching the opposite edge. Unfold.

PAPER TRICK

Amaze your friends by demonstrating that you can
walk through a sheet of A4 paper!

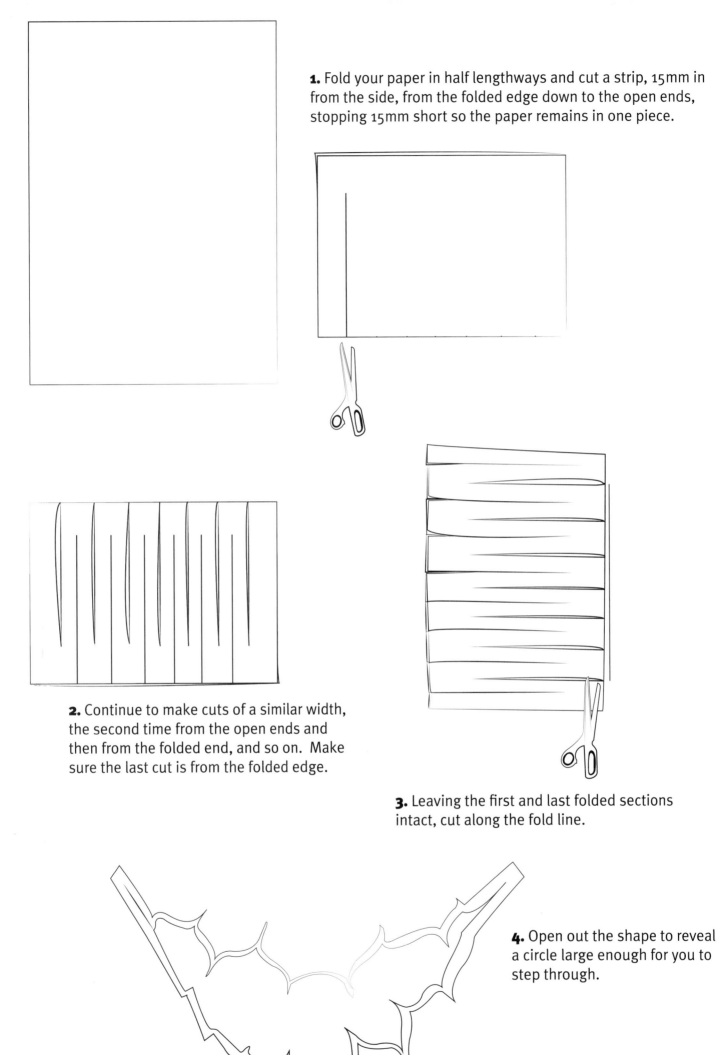

1. Fold your paper in half lengthways and cut a strip, 15mm in from the side, from the folded edge down to the open ends, stopping 15mm short so the paper remains in one piece.

2. Continue to make cuts of a similar width, the second time from the open ends and then from the folded end, and so on. Make sure the last cut is from the folded edge.

3. Leaving the first and last folded sections intact, cut along the fold line.

4. Open out the shape to reveal a circle large enough for you to step through.

PRESENT TAGS

1. Colour in the tags overleaf.

2. Write in your message.

3. Stick on your present.

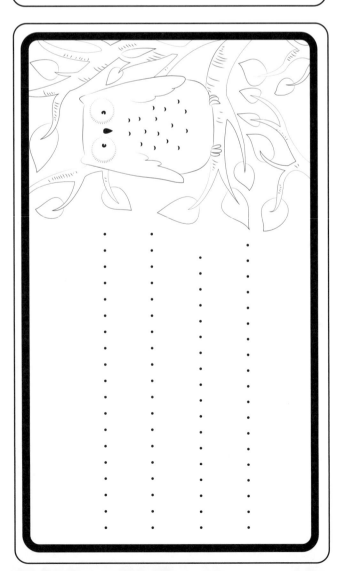

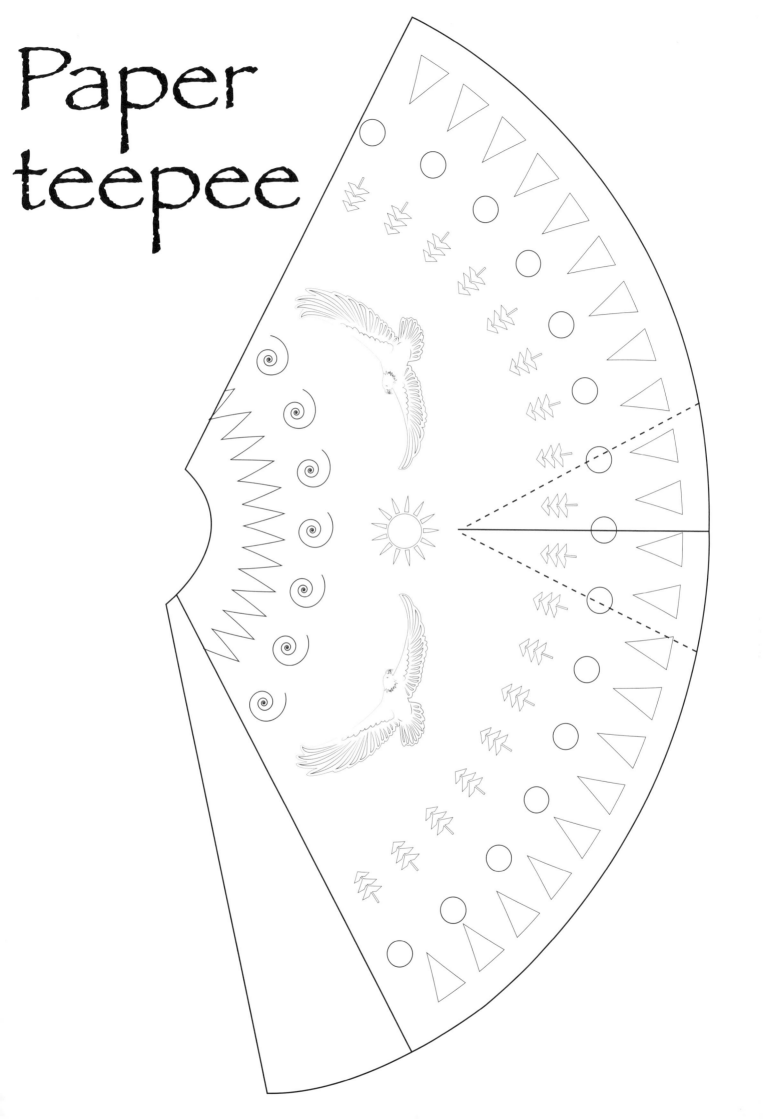

Paper
teepee

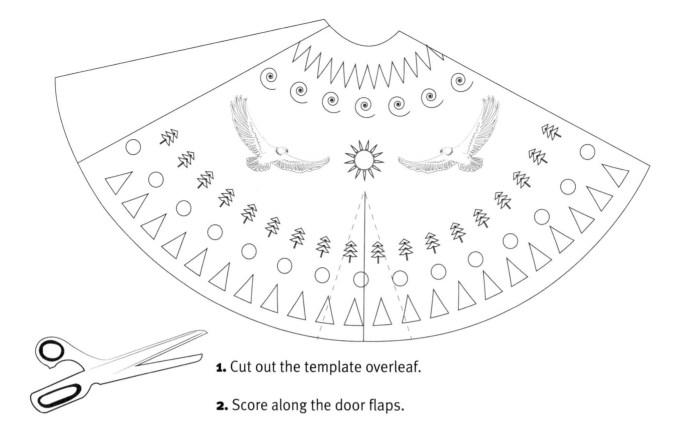

1. Cut out the template overleaf.

2. Score along the door flaps.

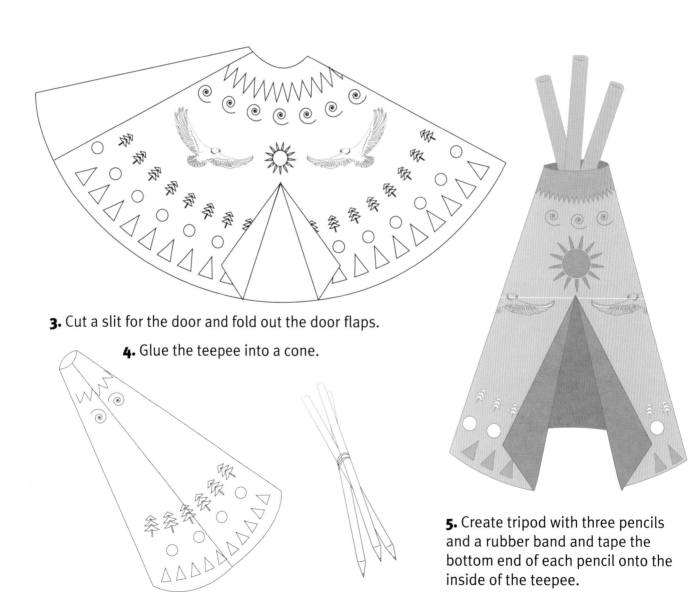

3. Cut a slit for the door and fold out the door flaps.

4. Glue the teepee into a cone.

5. Create tripod with three pencils and a rubber band and tape the bottom end of each pencil onto the inside of the teepee.

Paper Windmill

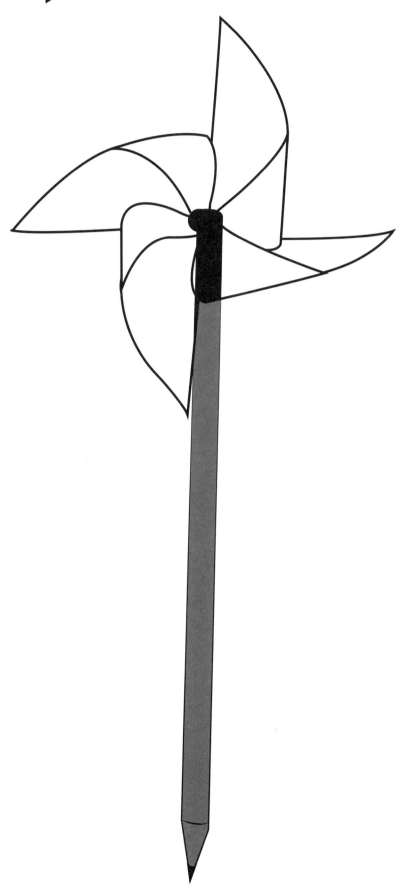

1. Cut a 15cm square of paper.

2. Fold the square in half diagonally and open out. Fold diagonally again, this time on the opposite diagonal and open out.

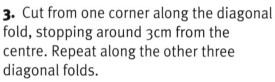

3. Cut from one corner along the diagonal fold, stopping around 3cm from the centre. Repeat along the other three diagonal folds.

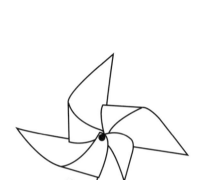

4. Fold alternate corners to the centre of the paper, securing with a dab of glue as you go.

5. Push a pin through the centre and out through the back of the windmill into the top of an eraser-tipped pencil.

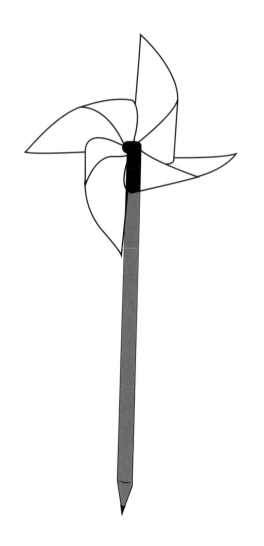

3D VALENTINE HEART

1. Cut out the 10 heart pairs.

2. Fold each pair in half. Without unfolding, apply glue to one of its outer faces.

3. Glue a second heart on top of the first one, aligning the two edges. Continue until you have used up all your hearts.

4. If you want to suspend your heart, cut a small length of paper to make a loop. Glue along the straight edge.

5. Glue the first and last heart faces together, sandwiching the loop in the middle.

Aeroplane

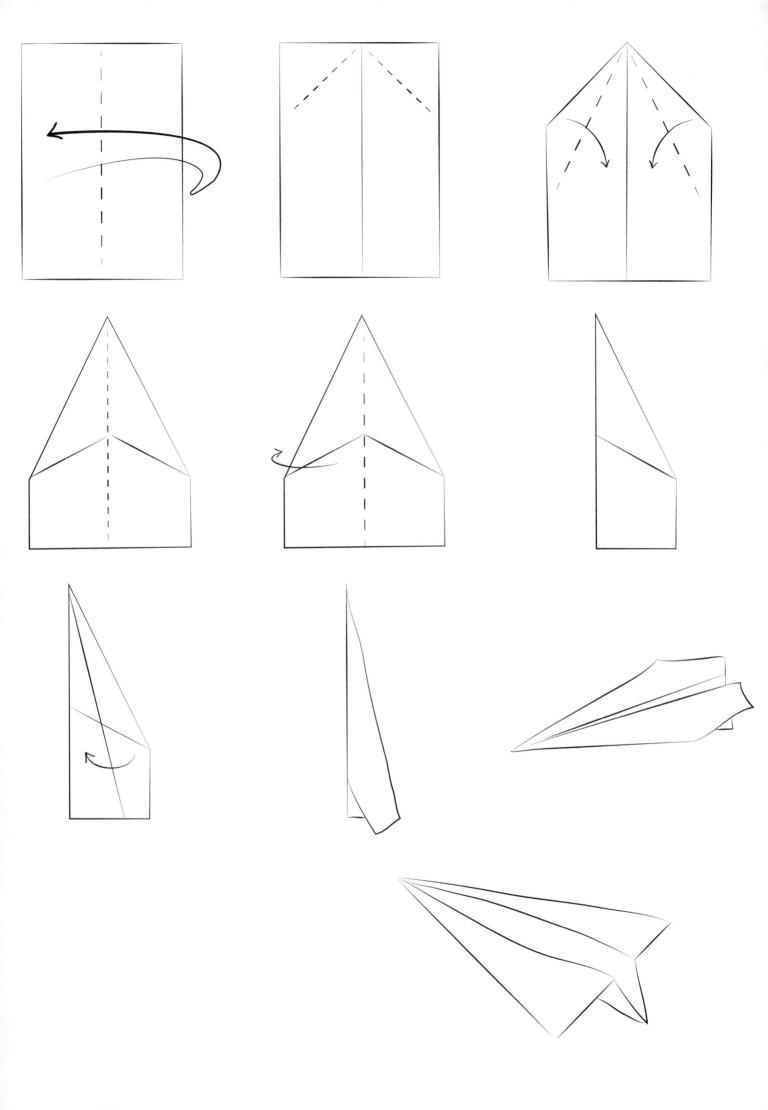

PAPER BOAT

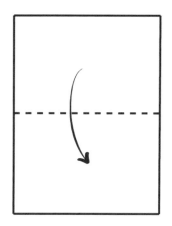

1. Fold the paper in half widthways.

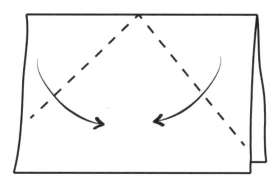

2. Fold the top corners to the centre.

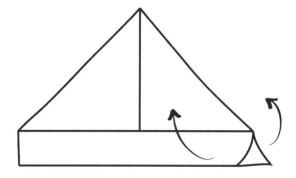

3. Fold up the strip at the bottom. Turn over and do the same the other side.

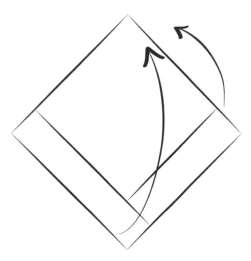

4. Open up to form a diamond.

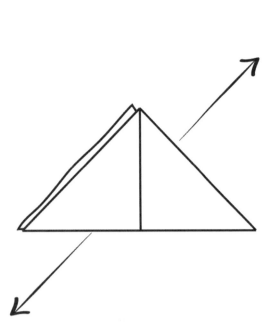

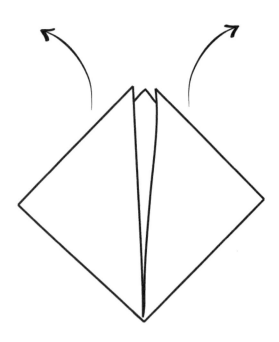

5. Fold up the bottom half. Turn over and do the same the other side.

6. Open up to form another (smaller) diamond.

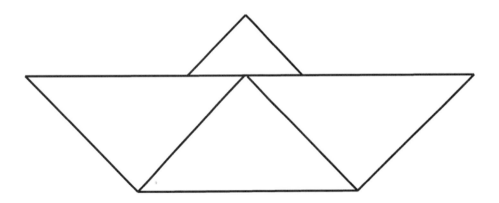

7. Pull out the sides to form your boat.

PLEATED FAN

1. Colour in the template overleaf, then cut out.

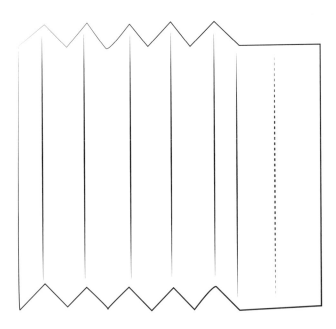

2. Fold the paper lengthways into pleats, accordian style. (Aim for 14 pleats.)

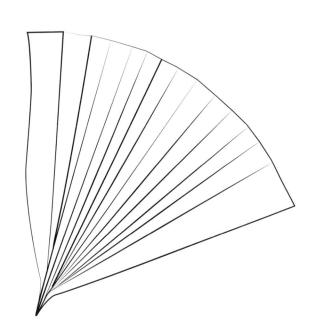

3. Pinch the pleats together 4cm in from one end and secure with a staple.

Origami
SWAN

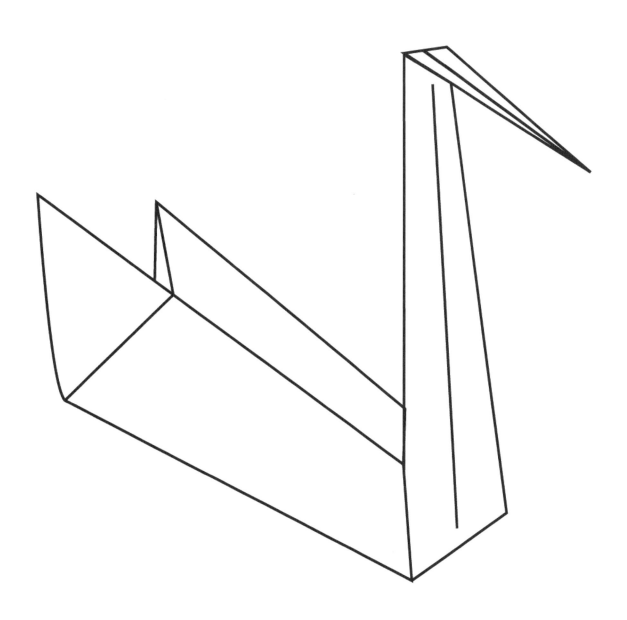

1. Make your sheet of paper into a square by folding the top left corner over to form a triangle. Cut off the rectangle below the triangle you just formed.

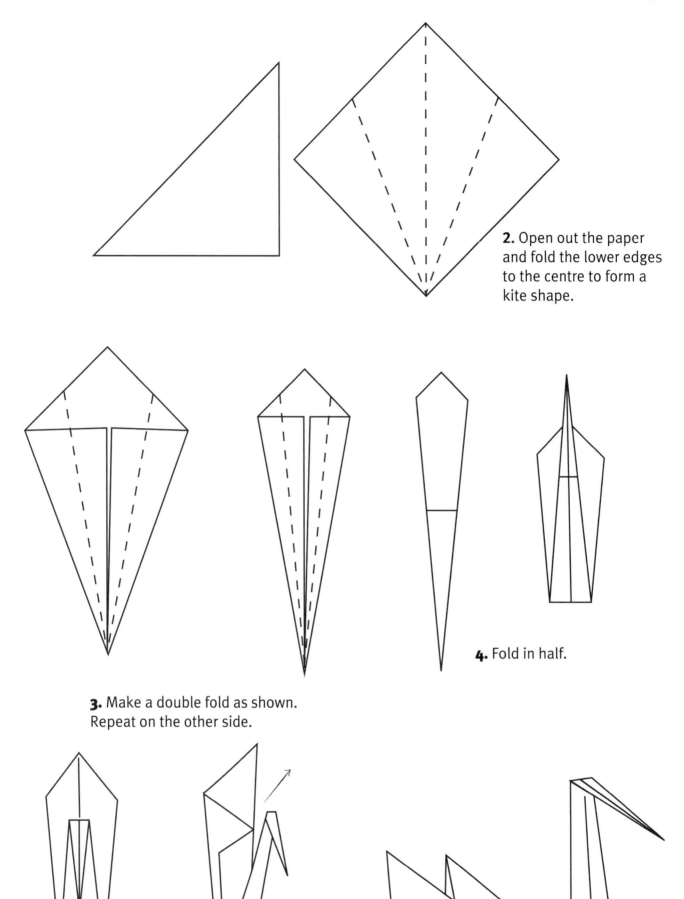

2. Open out the paper and fold the lower edges to the centre to form a kite shape.

3. Make a double fold as shown. Repeat on the other side.

4. Fold in half.

5. Fold down the head of the swan.

Pleated butterfly

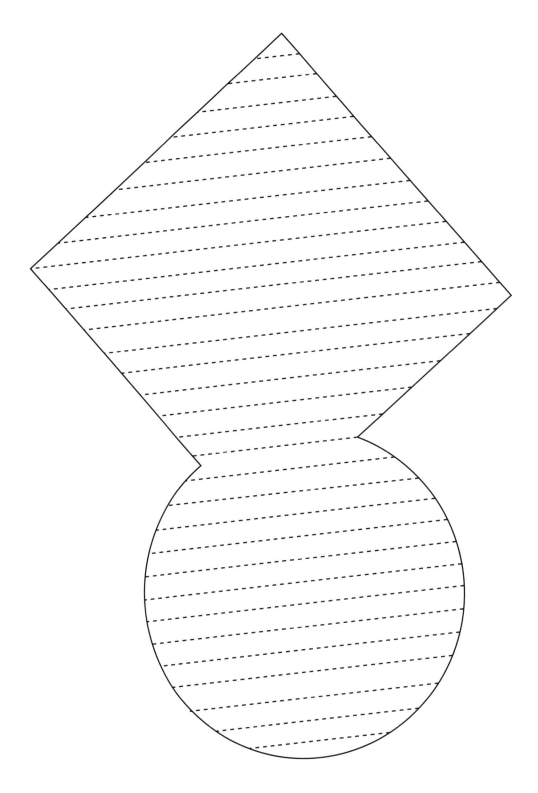

1. Cut out the template, then fold accordian-style along the lines marked.

2. Squeeze the paper in the middle and then wrap an elastic band around the middle section.

3. Gently open up the wings on either side of the elastic band. If you like, you can glue a strip of paper over the elastic band to cover it.

Paper Rosettes

1. You will need three sheets of paper. Take one sheet and fold widthways, accordion-style, six times. Repeat with the other two sheets of paper.

2. Fold each in half and join in the middle with double-sided tape.

3. Join the three fans together in the same way.

4. Decorate the middle with flowers.

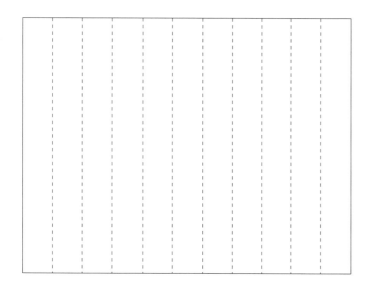

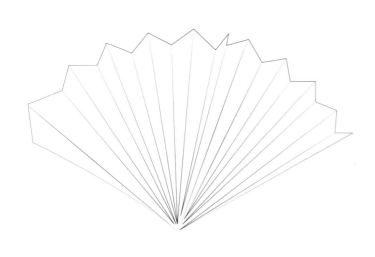

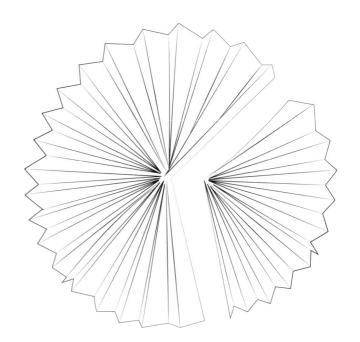

FOLDED BRACELET

1. Cut your paper into strips measuring 12cm x 3cm.

2. Fold each strip in half lengthways, then in half widthways.

3. Take two folded pieces and slip one inside the other, with the open end of the inside piece at the bottom. Make sure that the section of paper sticking out at the top is a little larger than the width of the pieces of paper.

4. Fold one half of the open end of the inside paper to the left at a right angle, as shown.

5. Then fold it up on top of the outer strip of paper.

6. Turn the paper over and do the same on the other side, but this time fold the open end of the inside paper to the right and then up. Secure each folded up piece in place with glue or tape.

7. Turn on its side and add a new piece of folded paper through the loop you've just created. Again, make sure that the section sticking out at the top is a little larger than the width of the pieces of paper.

8. Fold one half of the open end of the inside piece of paper to the left, then up. Tuck the end into the pocket created by the previous strip. Turn over and do the same on the other side but this time fold the open end of the inside piece of paper to the right and then up before tucking in.

9. Turn the bracelet to the right and continue.

10. Keep adding strips until the bracelet is long enough (make a necklace if you prefer). When you've reached the length you want, slot the first strip into the last loop and tuck down into the pocket. Do the same with the inside tail.

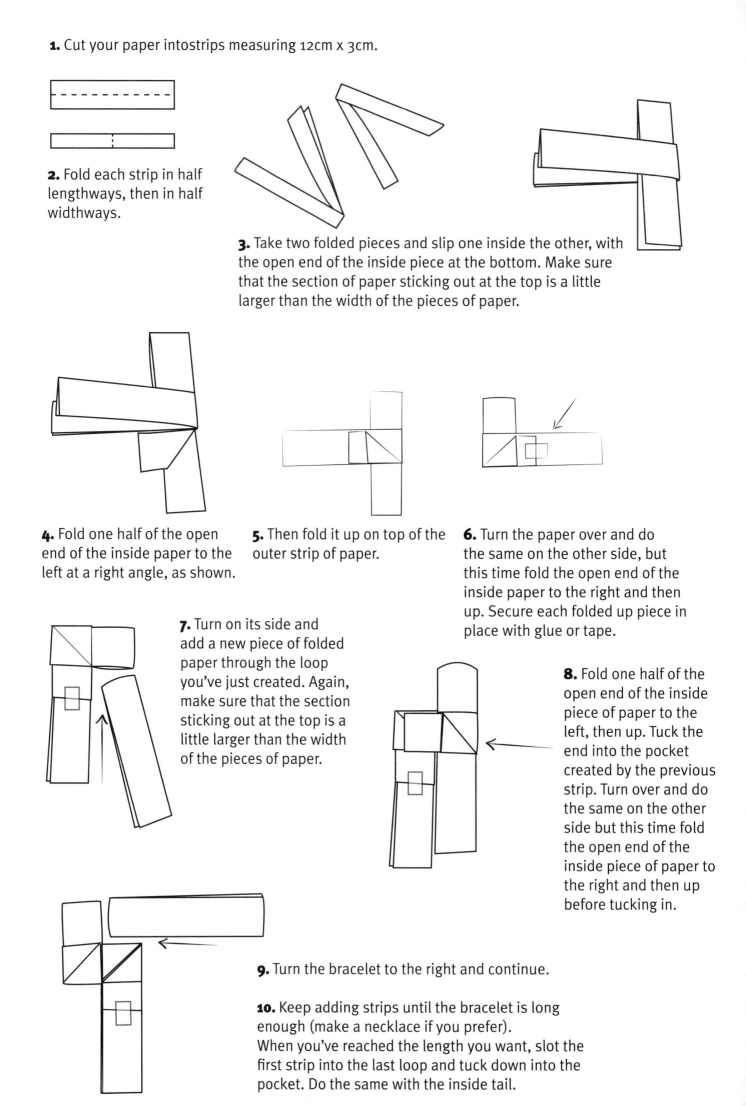

PAPER CUP

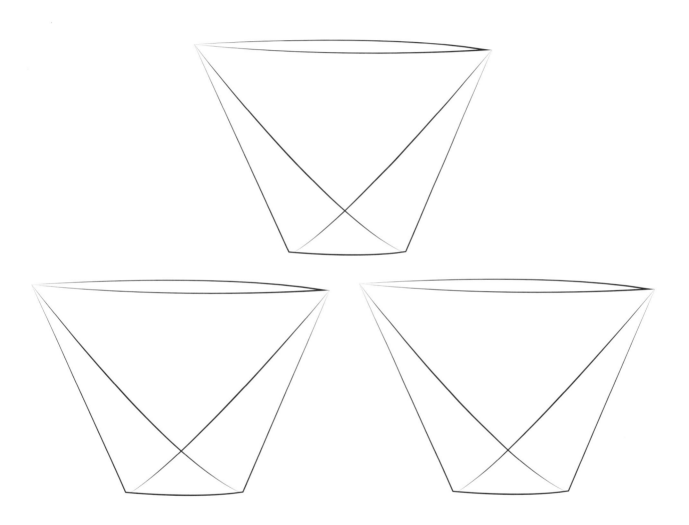

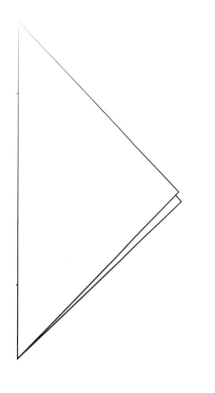

1. Make your sheet of paper into a square by folding the top corner over to form a triangle. Cut off the rectangle below the triangle you just formed.

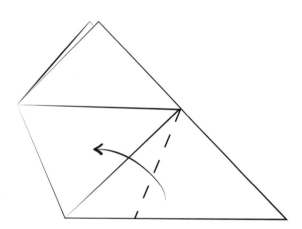

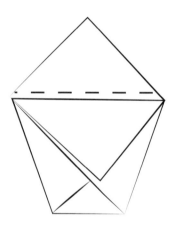

3. Turn the triangle so that the longest edge is at the bottom and fold in the bottom corners of the triangle on an angle so that their points meet the opposite edge, as shown.

4. Fold down the two triangular flaps at the top and open up the cup.

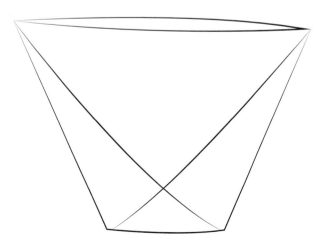

Origami
HEART

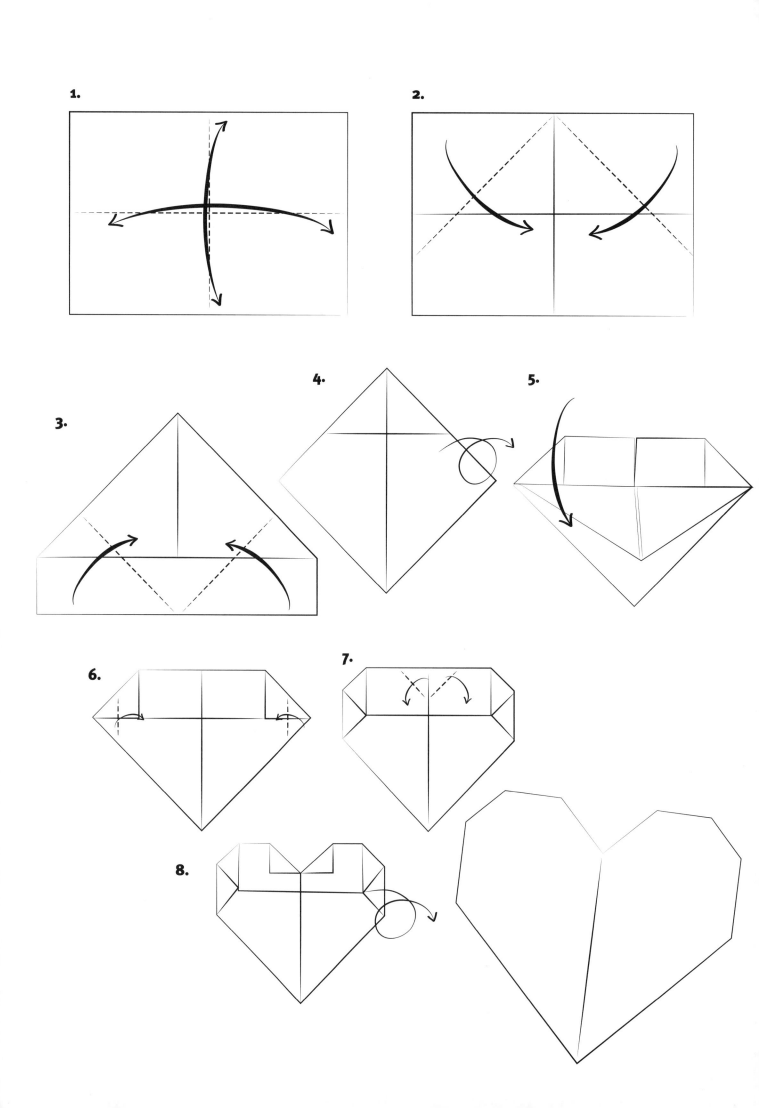

Origami
FLOWER

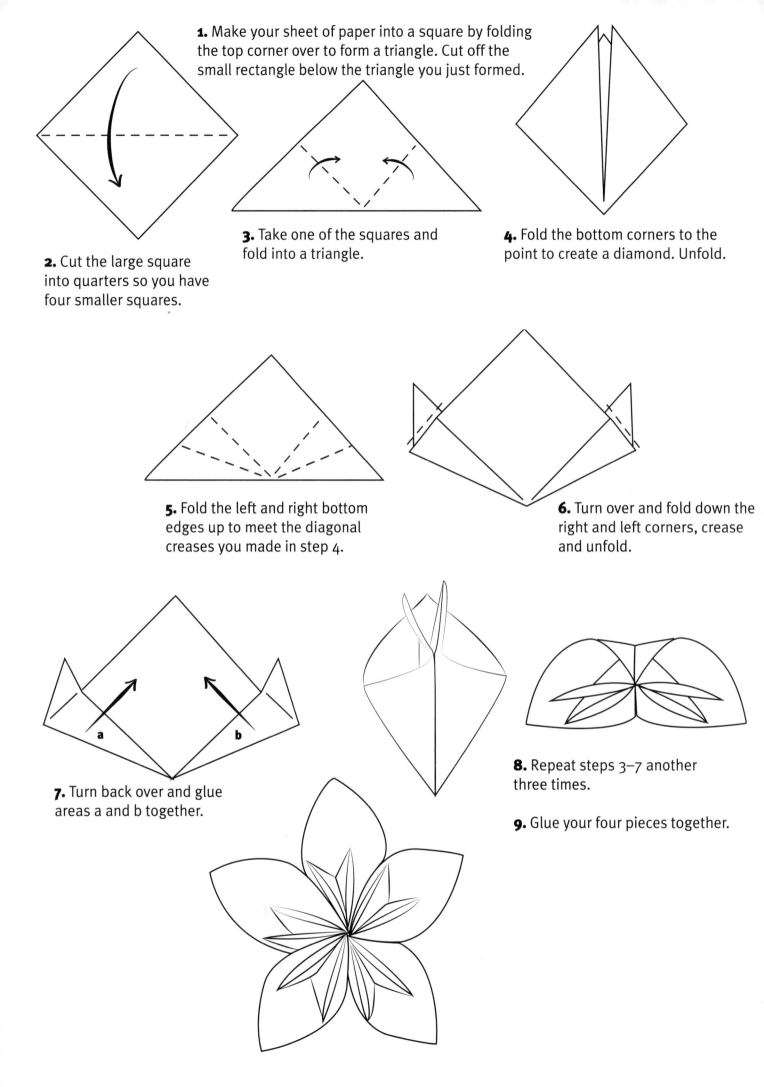

1. Make your sheet of paper into a square by folding the top corner over to form a triangle. Cut off the small rectangle below the triangle you just formed.

2. Cut the large square into quarters so you have four smaller squares.

3. Take one of the squares and fold into a triangle.

4. Fold the bottom corners to the point to create a diamond. Unfold.

5. Fold the left and right bottom edges up to meet the diagonal creases you made in step 4.

6. Turn over and fold down the right and left corners, crease and unfold.

7. Turn back over and glue areas a and b together.

8. Repeat steps 3–7 another three times.

9. Glue your four pieces together.

Origami
FISH

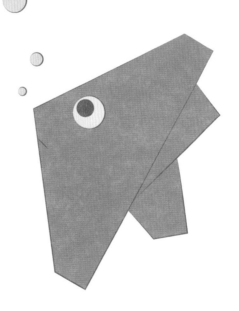

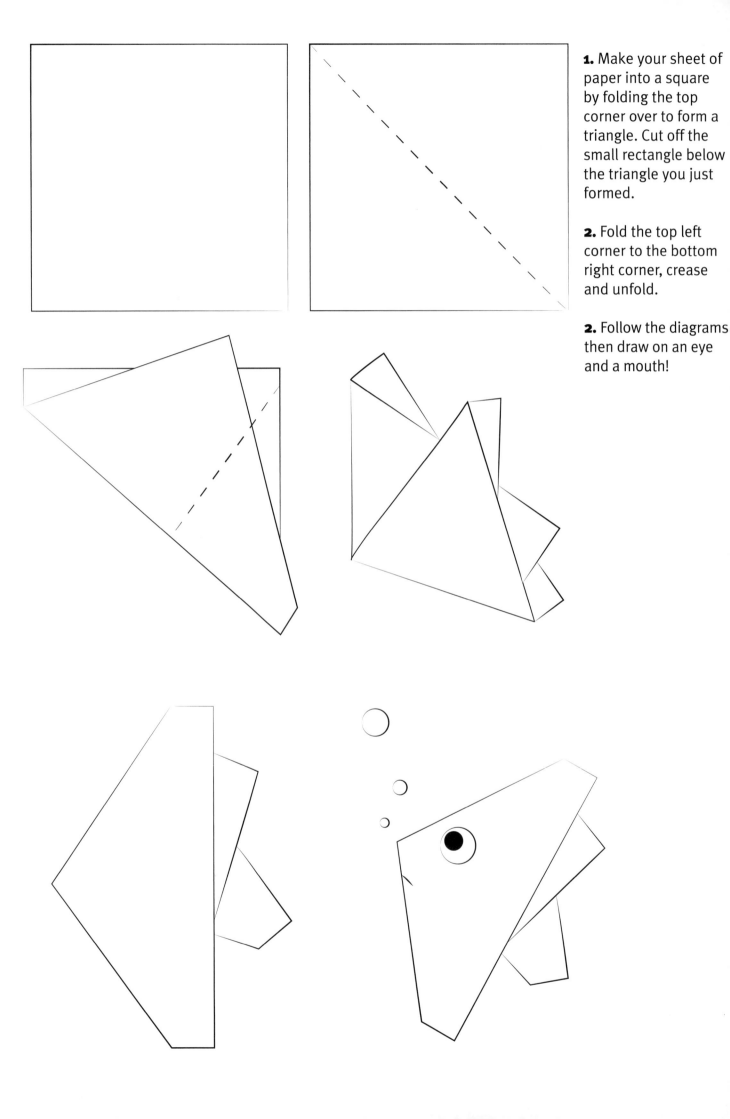

1. Make your sheet of paper into a square by folding the top corner over to form a triangle. Cut off the small rectangle below the triangle you just formed.

2. Fold the top left corner to the bottom right corner, crease and unfold.

2. Follow the diagrams then draw on an eye and a mouth!

SIMPLE
BOX

1. Colour in the box.

2. Cut out.

3. Score along the dotted lines.

4. Glue along the flaps and stick together.

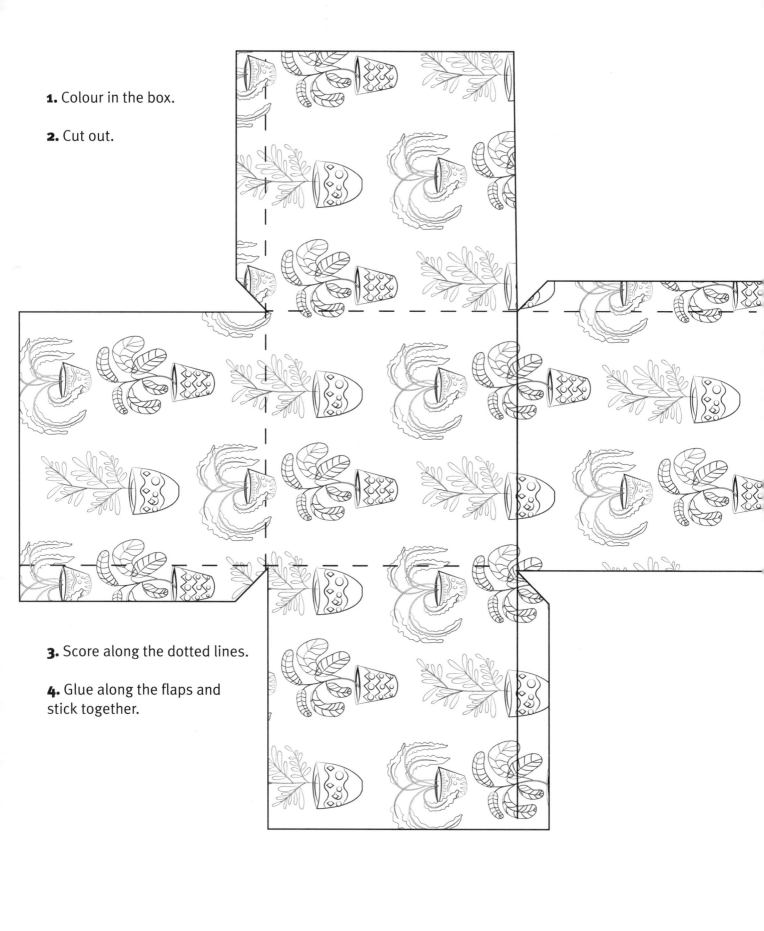

PAPER DICE

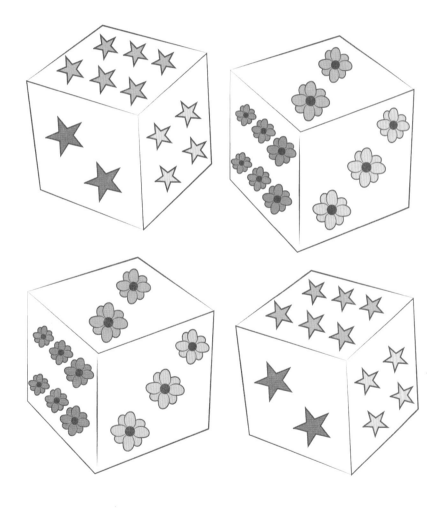

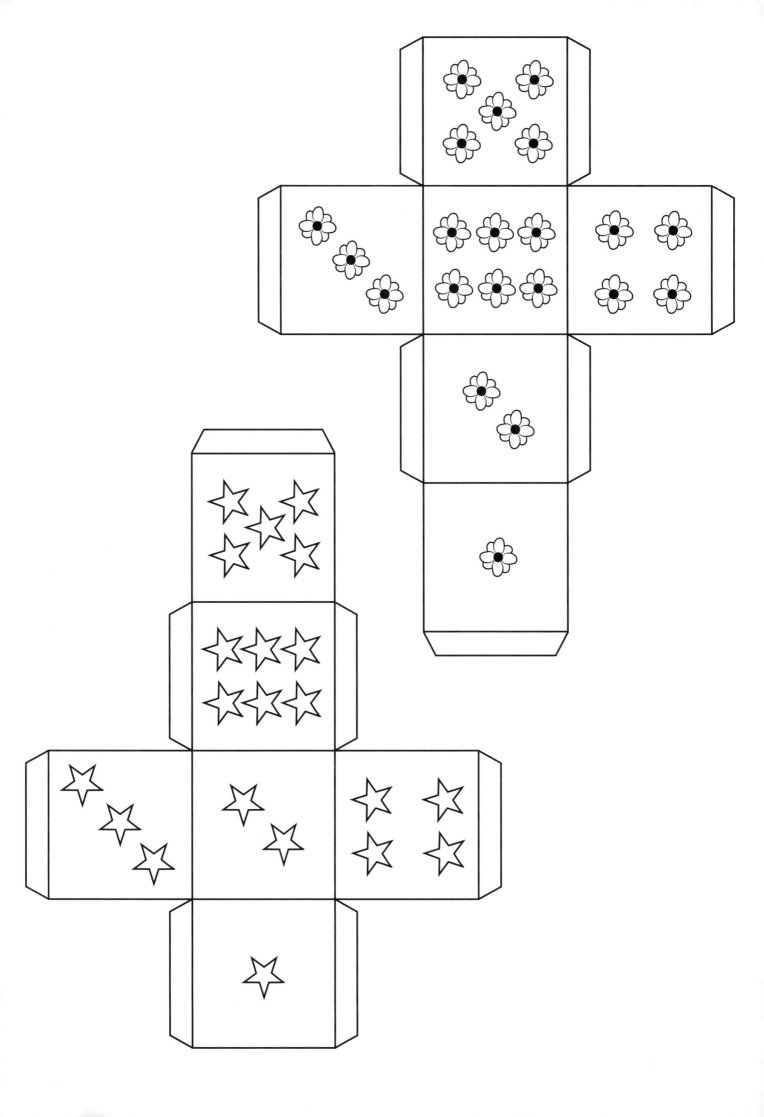

Rectangular box
with lid

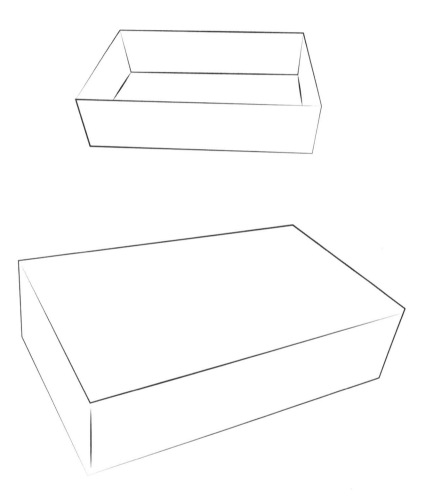

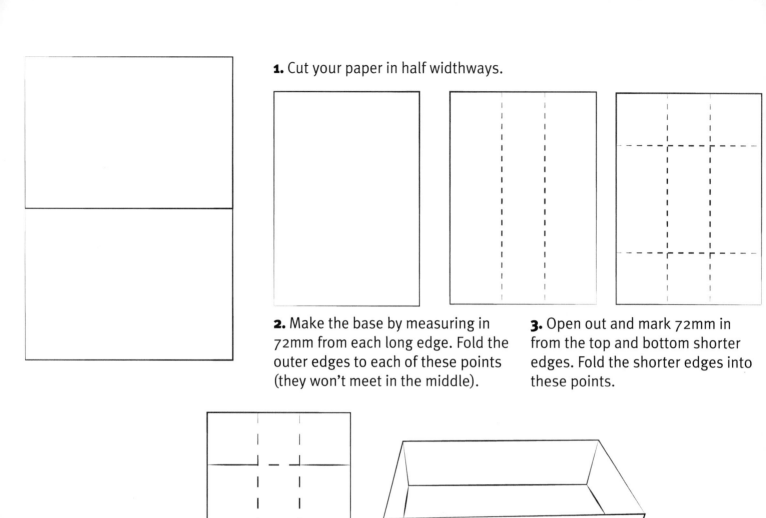

1. Cut your paper in half widthways.

2. Make the base by measuring in 72mm from each long edge. Fold the outer edges to each of these points (they won't meet in the middle).

3. Open out and mark 72mm in from the top and bottom shorter edges. Fold the shorter edges into these points.

4. Open out and make a cut in from the corners, as shown.

5. Fold up into a box shape and secure either with glue or staples.

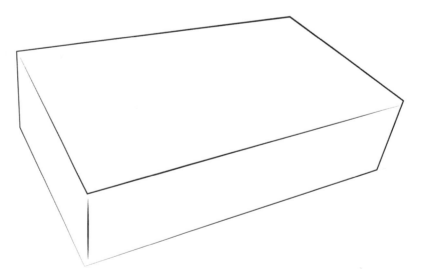

6. Make the lid in the same way as the base, but measure in 70mm rather than 72mm.

PAPER HOUSE

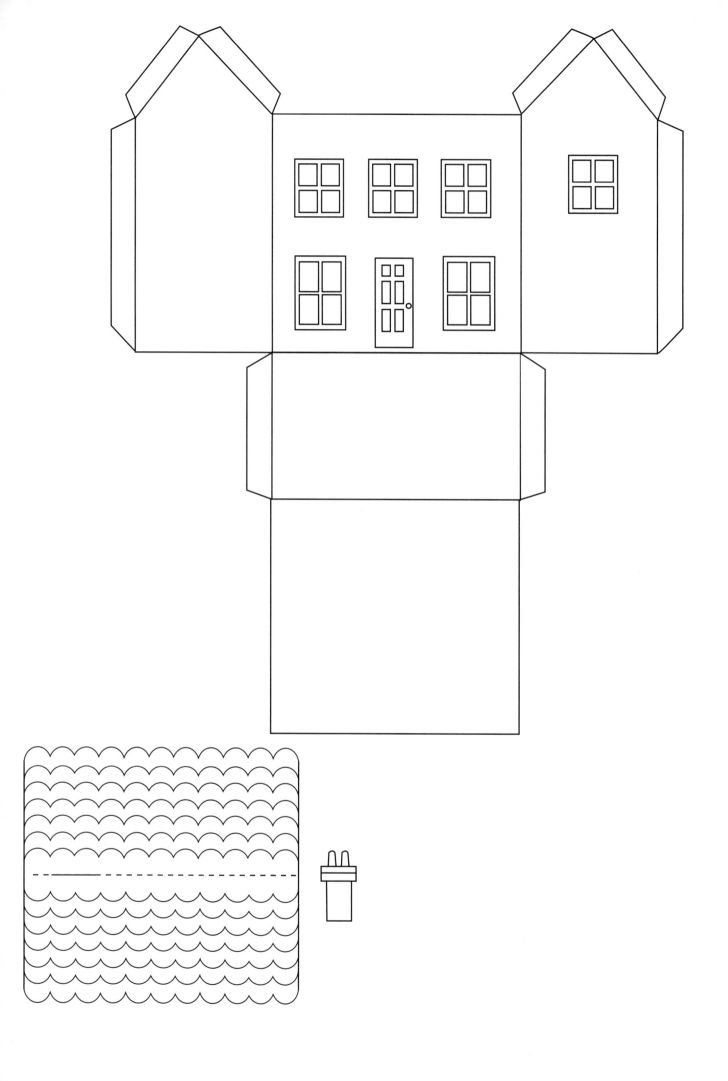

Paper
water balloon

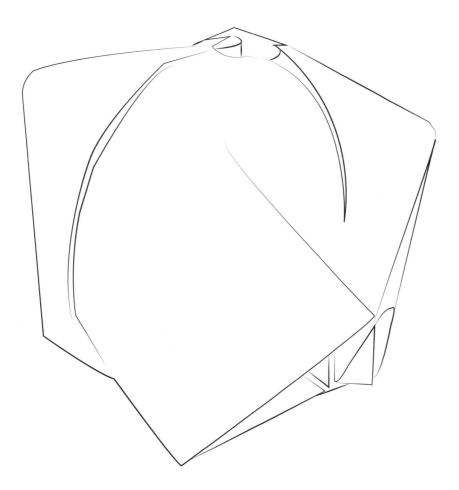

1. Make your sheet of paper into a square by
folding the top corner over to form a triangle.
Cut off the rectangle below the triangle
you just formed.

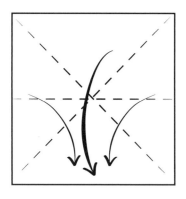

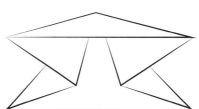

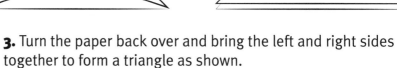

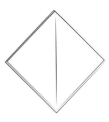

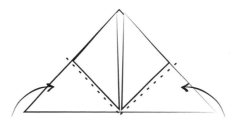

2. Fold in half diagonally, crease and unfold. Repeat on the other diagonal. Flip the paper over and fold in half horizontally.

3. Turn the paper back over and bring the left and right sides together to form a triangle as shown.

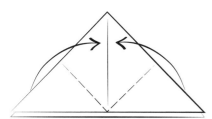

4. Fold the front bottom corners up to the point at the top as shown. Flip the paper over and to the same on the other side to create a diamond.

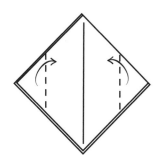

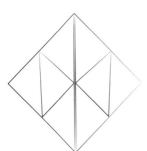

5. Fold the horizontal corners to the centre on both sides.

6. Open up each of the four 'pockets' and tuck in the flaps below.

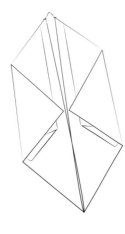

7. Expand the balloon, first by partially unfolding and then by blowing gently into the hole at one end.

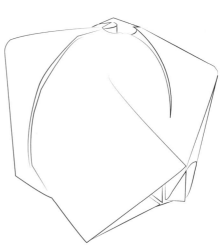

Fortune teller

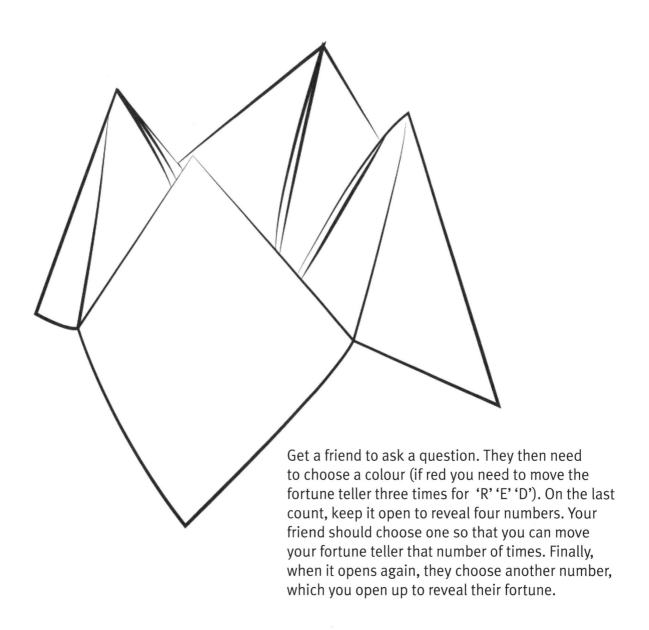

Get a friend to ask a question. They then need to choose a colour (if red you need to move the fortune teller three times for 'R' 'E' 'D'). On the last count, keep it open to reveal four numbers. Your friend should choose one so that you can move your fortune teller that number of times. Finally, when it opens again, they choose another number, which you open up to reveal their fortune.

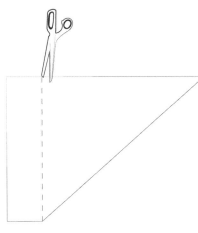

1. Make your sheet of paper into a square by folding the top right-hand corner over to form a triangle. Cut off the rectangle.

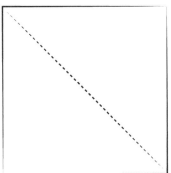

2. Make a diagonal crease.

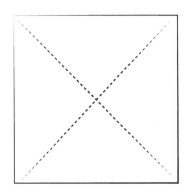

3. Turn the paper 45 degrees and make another diagonal crease.

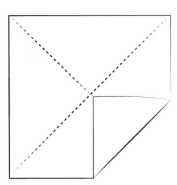

4. Fold the bottom right-hand corner to the centre.

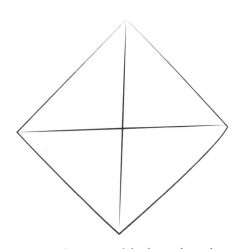

5. Repeat with the other three corners.

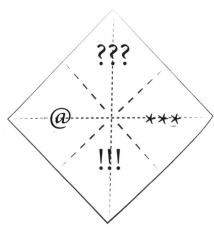

6. Flip the square over and write your fortunes in the eight triangles (Yes, Maybe, No chance, etc.)

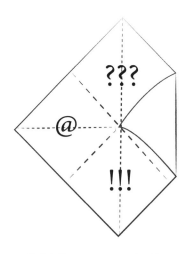

7. Fold the corners in the centre.

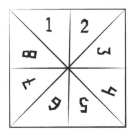

8. Write numbers on the eight triangles

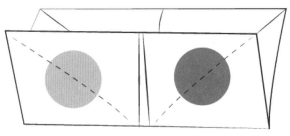

9. Turn the square over and add a coloured dot to each of the four triangular flaps.

10. Prise these flaps open so you can fit your thumb and index finger from each hand.

Chinese Lantern

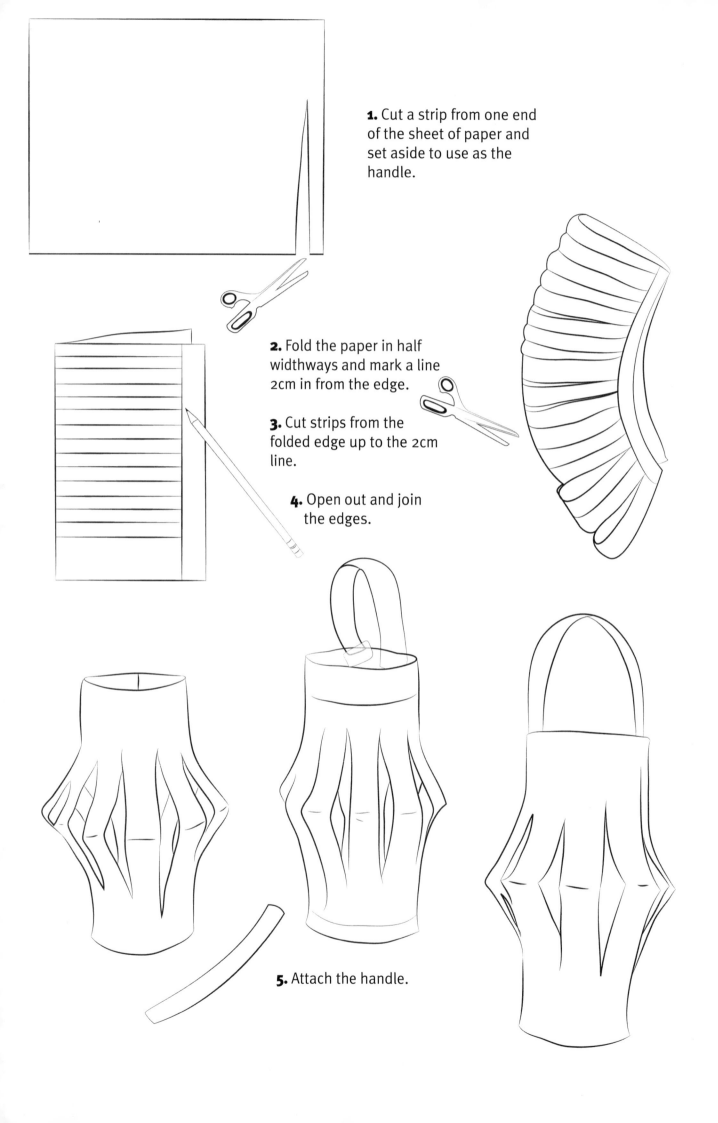

1. Cut a strip from one end of the sheet of paper and set aside to use as the handle.

2. Fold the paper in half widthways and mark a line 2cm in from the edge.

3. Cut strips from the folded edge up to the 2cm line.

4. Open out and join the edges.

5. Attach the handle.

Paper frames

Cut out the frames overleaf and use to adorn your photos.

Paper Chain
Hearts

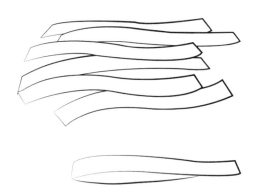

1. Cut the paper lengthways into 7 strips.

2. Fold your first strip in half.

3. Bend the two cut ends into a heart shape and secure with either a staple or glue.

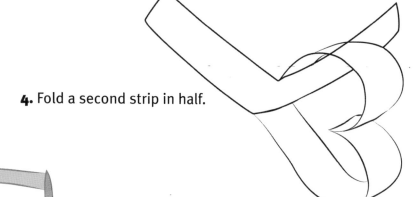

4. Fold a second strip in half.

5. Link through the heart, bend the two cut ends into another heart shape, and secure. Continue until you've used all your strips/ have the length of chain you want.

Easter Bunny Garland

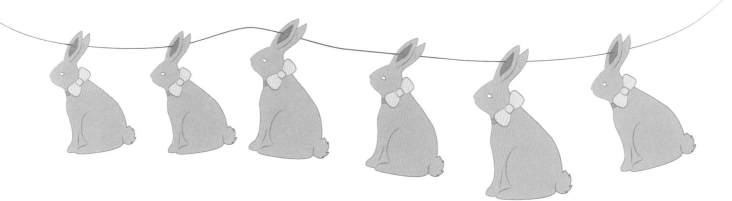

Easter basket

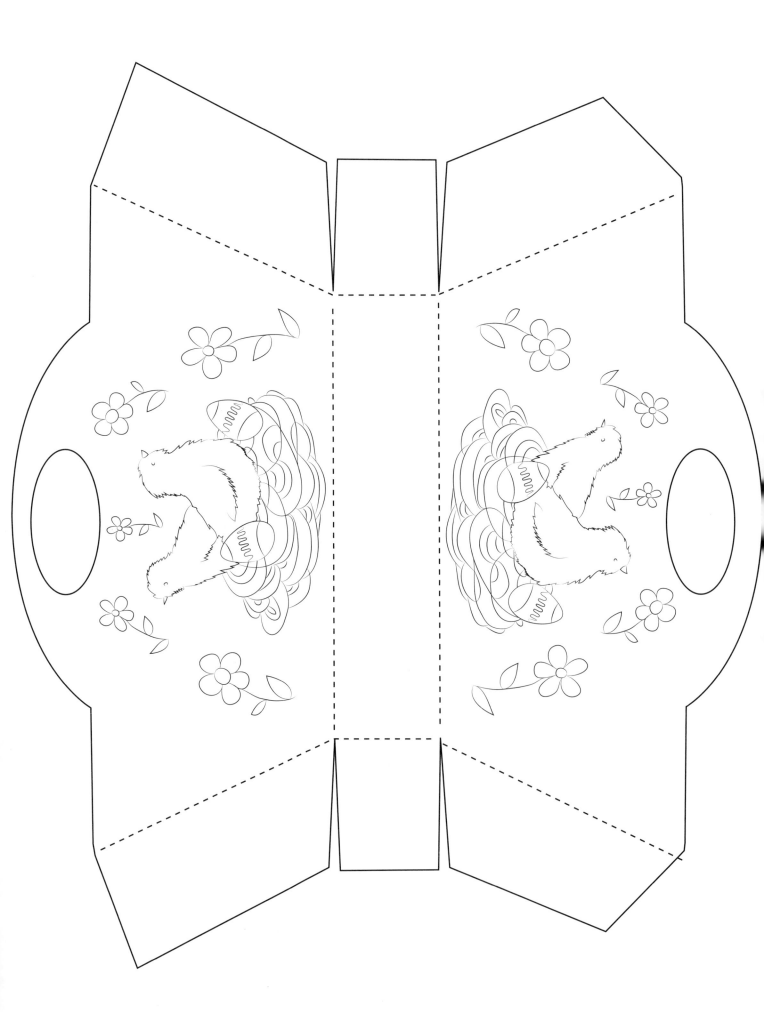

FLOWERS

1. Cut out the flowers.

2. Place a dab of glue in the centre of the largest flower. Lay the next largest on top, at a slight angle to the first. Repeat with the remaining flowers.

Witch Shadow Puppet

1. Cut out the stencil and attach it to a pencil.

2. To create your puppet show, you will need a screen (through which light must be able to pass) on which to project the shadows. This screen can be another sheet of paper. The light (the sun or a lamp) must shine on to the screen. Anything placed between the light source and the screen will cast a shadow.

HALLOWEEN PAPER CHAINS

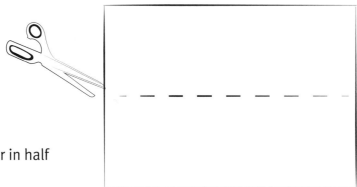

1. Cut your sheet of paper in half lengthways.

2. Fold each half into quarters, accordion style.

3. Draw your figure on the top layers, making sure that two parts extend beyond the edges.

4. Cut out, unfold and connect the chains using glue or sticky tape.

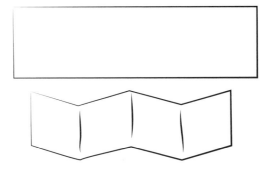

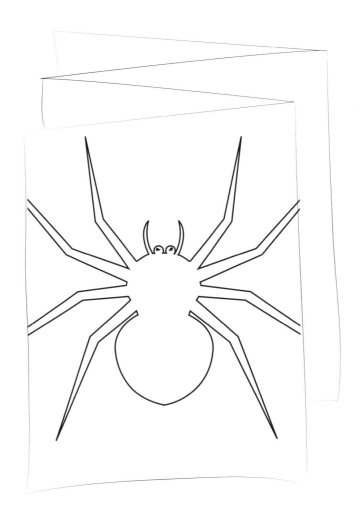

Halloween Bats

1. Cut out and attach to thread.

2. Hang wherever they will frighten your friends.

Cone Treat Holder

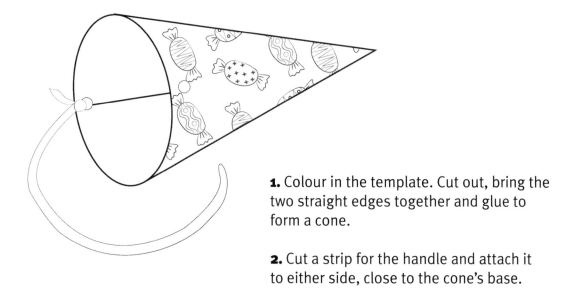

1. Colour in the template. Cut out, bring the two straight edges together and glue to form a cone.

2. Cut a strip for the handle and attach it to either side, close to the cone's base.

curved hanging decoration

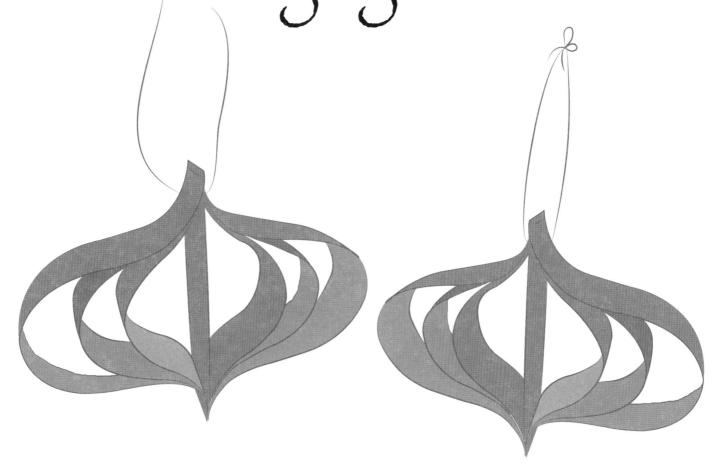

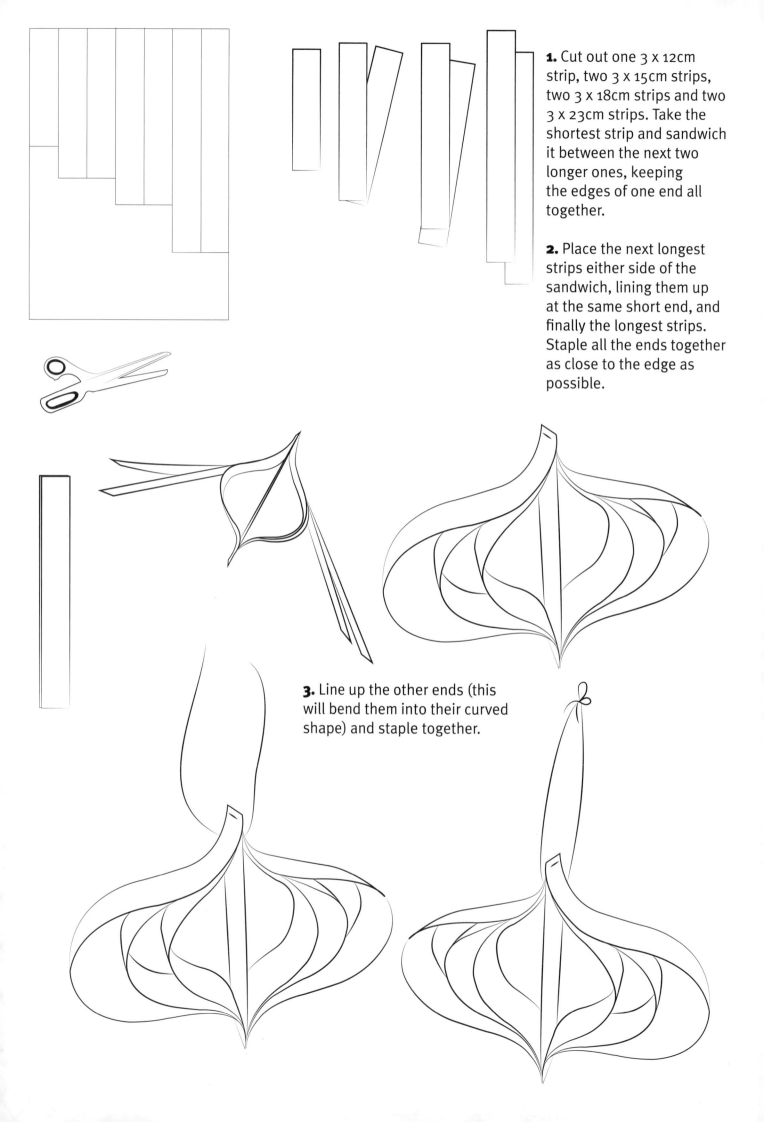

1. Cut out one 3 x 12cm strip, two 3 x 15cm strips, two 3 x 18cm strips and two 3 x 23cm strips. Take the shortest strip and sandwich it between the next two longer ones, keeping the edges of one end all together.

2. Place the next longest strips either side of the sandwich, lining them up at the same short end, and finally the longest strips. Staple all the ends together as close to the edge as possible.

3. Line up the other ends (this will bend them into their curved shape) and staple together.

Paper Chains

1. Colour in the templates overleaf (photocopy to make a longer chain). Cut along the dotted lines.
2. Paste, tape or staple the ends of the first strip to form a loop.
3. Link the next strip through the loop and secure as before. Continue with the remaining strips.

Folded tree

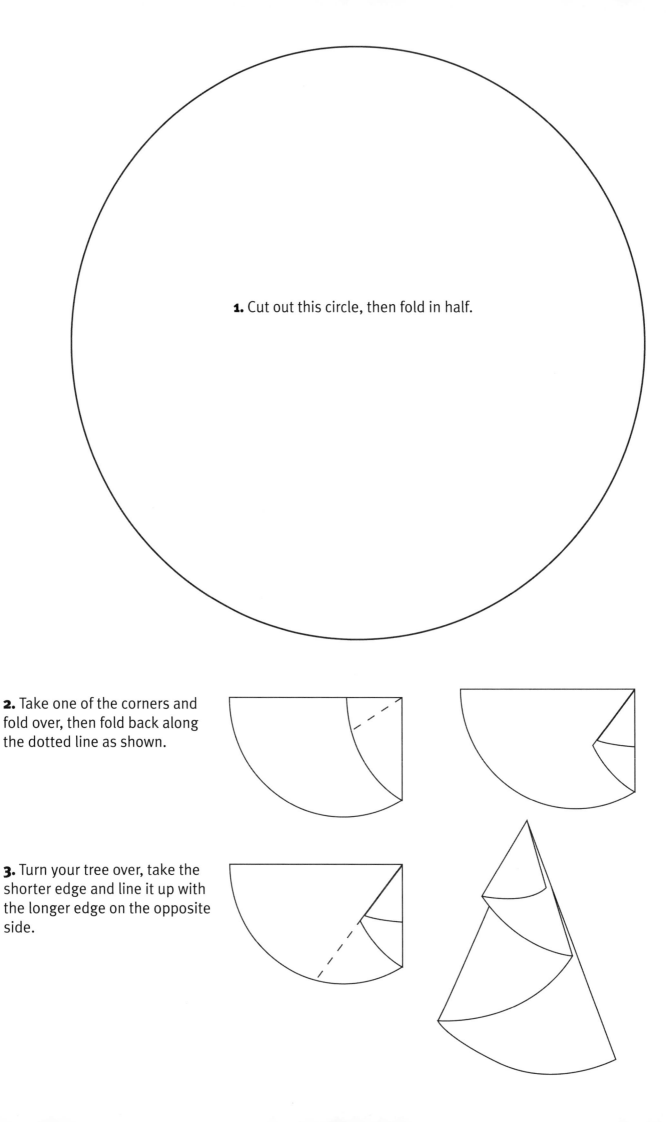

1. Cut out this circle, then fold in half.

2. Take one of the corners and fold over, then fold back along the dotted line as shown.

3. Turn your tree over, take the shorter edge and line it up with the longer edge on the opposite side.

Christmas Wreath

1. Cut out the circular template overleaf. This is the base onto which you stick the leaves.

2. Cut out as many leaves as you think necessary (the more you have the fuller your wreath will be). Glue in place.

CHRISTMAS BAUBLES

Flying Angels

1. Colour in your angels.

2. Cut out, attach to a thread and hang on a Christmas tree, or along a mantelpiece or window.

3D STAR

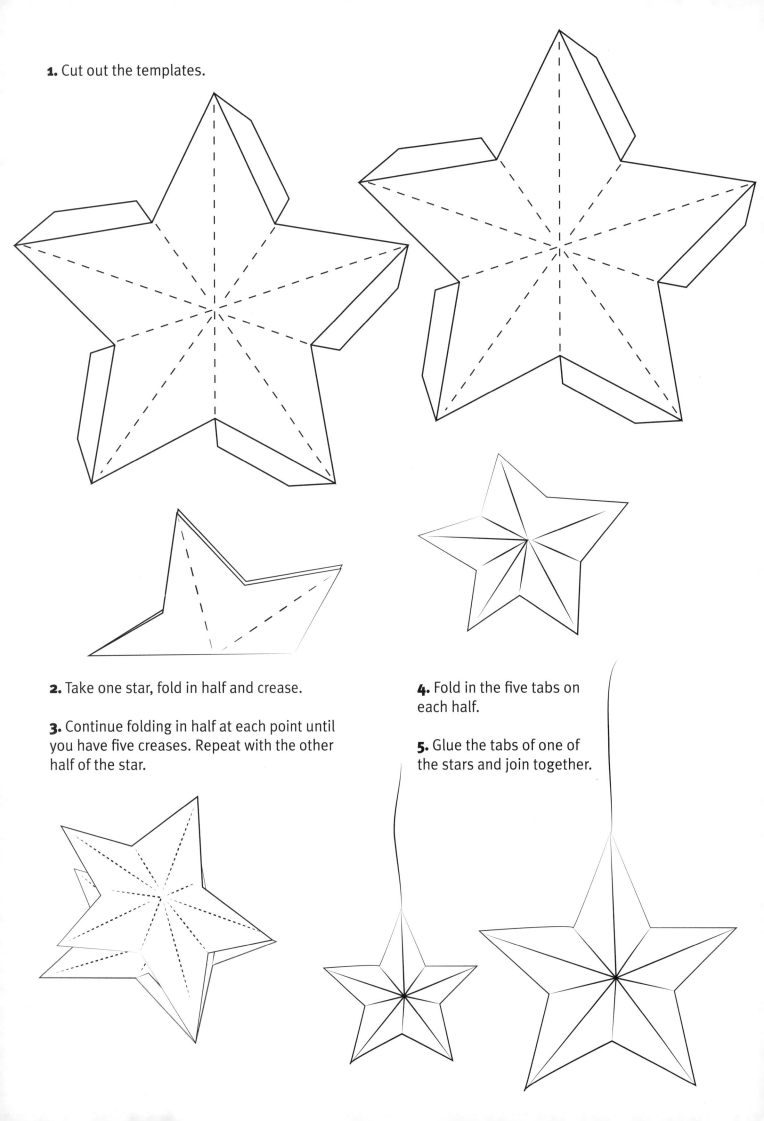

1. Cut out the templates.

2. Take one star, fold in half and crease.

3. Continue folding in half at each point until you have five creases. Repeat with the other half of the star.

4. Fold in the five tabs on each half.

5. Glue the tabs of one of the stars and join together.

Reindeer Stencil

Cut out the template overleaf using a craft knife.

Skater Stencil

Cut out the template overleaf using a craft knife.

Folded and cut
snowflake

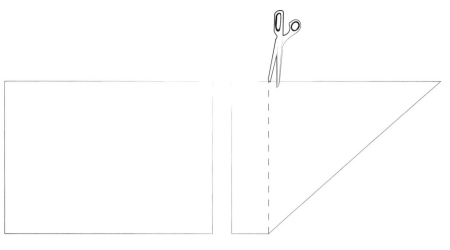

1. Make your sheet of paper into a square by folding the top corner paper over to form a triangle. Cut off the small rectangle below the triangle you just formed.

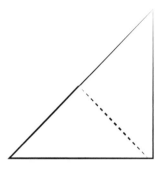

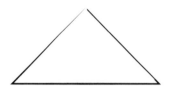

2. Fold the triangle in half by bringing the bottom left-hand corner to meet the top right corner. Fold once more to make a smaller triangle.

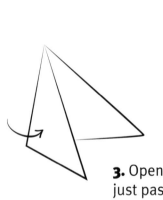

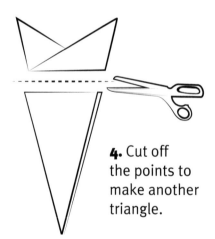

3. Open it out once and fold the left-hand edge in to the just past the centre fold. Fold the right-hand edge in in the same way to create the shape shown above.

4. Cut off the points to make another triangle.

5. Cut out a design of your choice from each side. Open up.

Mini Bunting

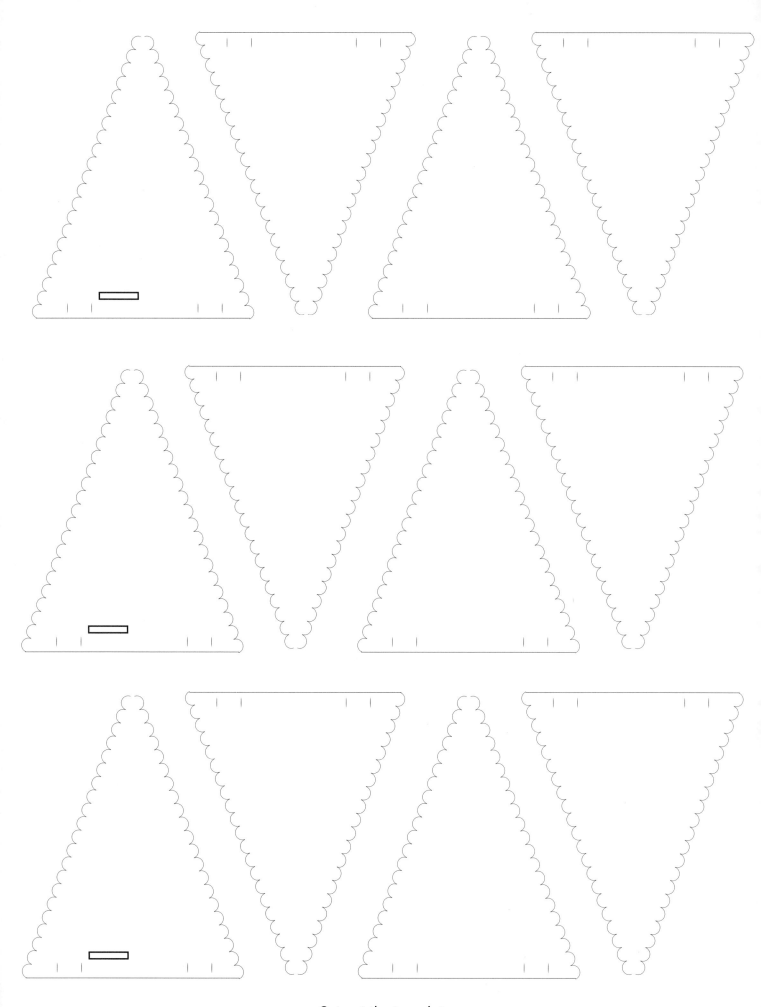

1. Cut out the templates.

2. Cut slits where marked and thread through a ribbon so you can hang up.

Stencil Bunting

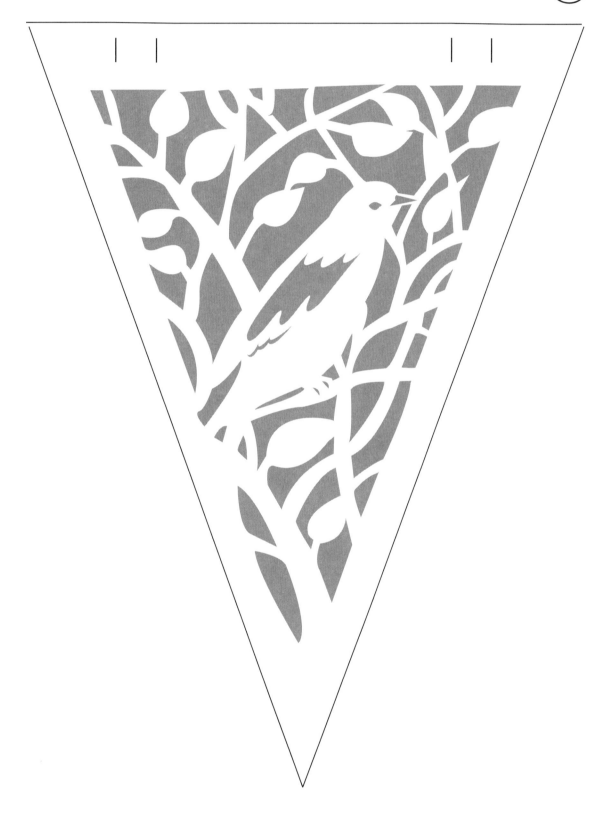

Either colour in or cut out the shaded areas using a craft knife.

FOX MASK

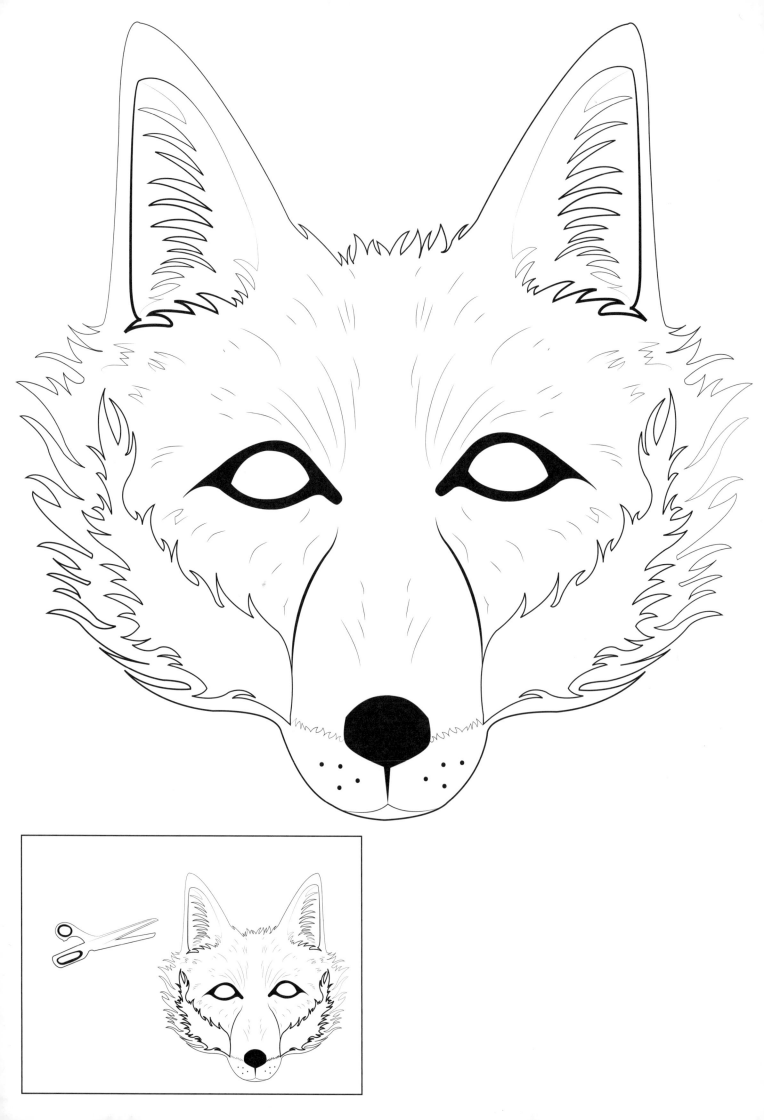

Venetian Mask

Bandit Mask

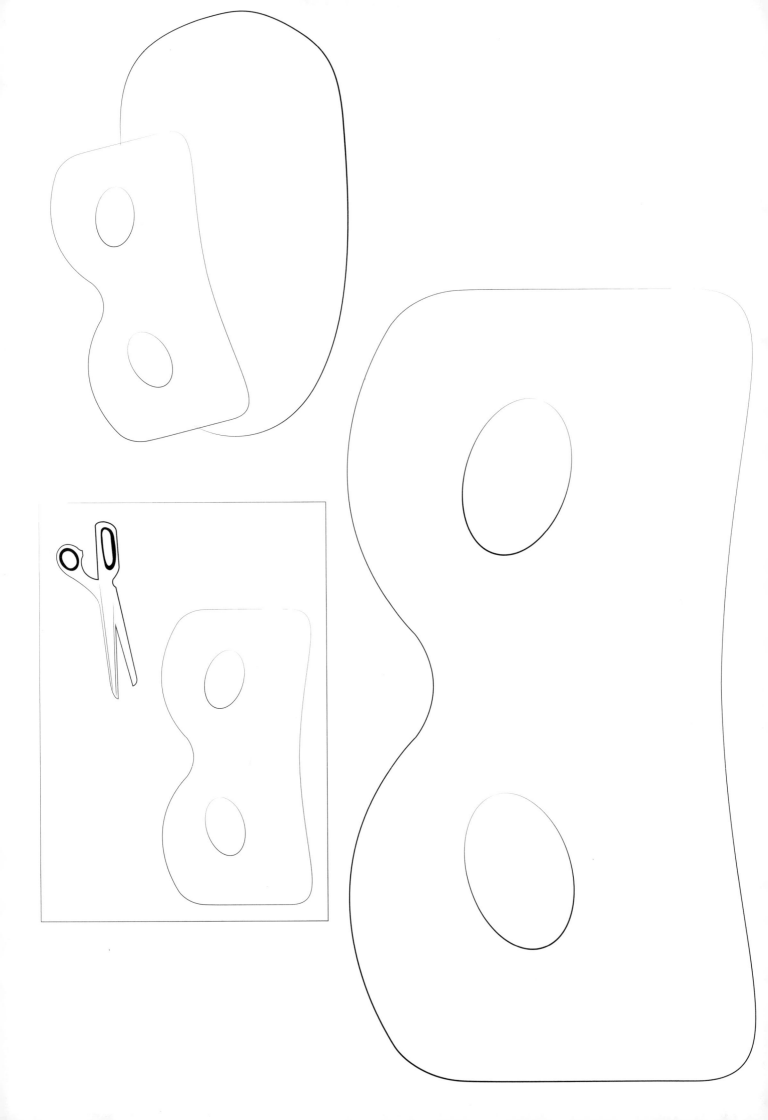

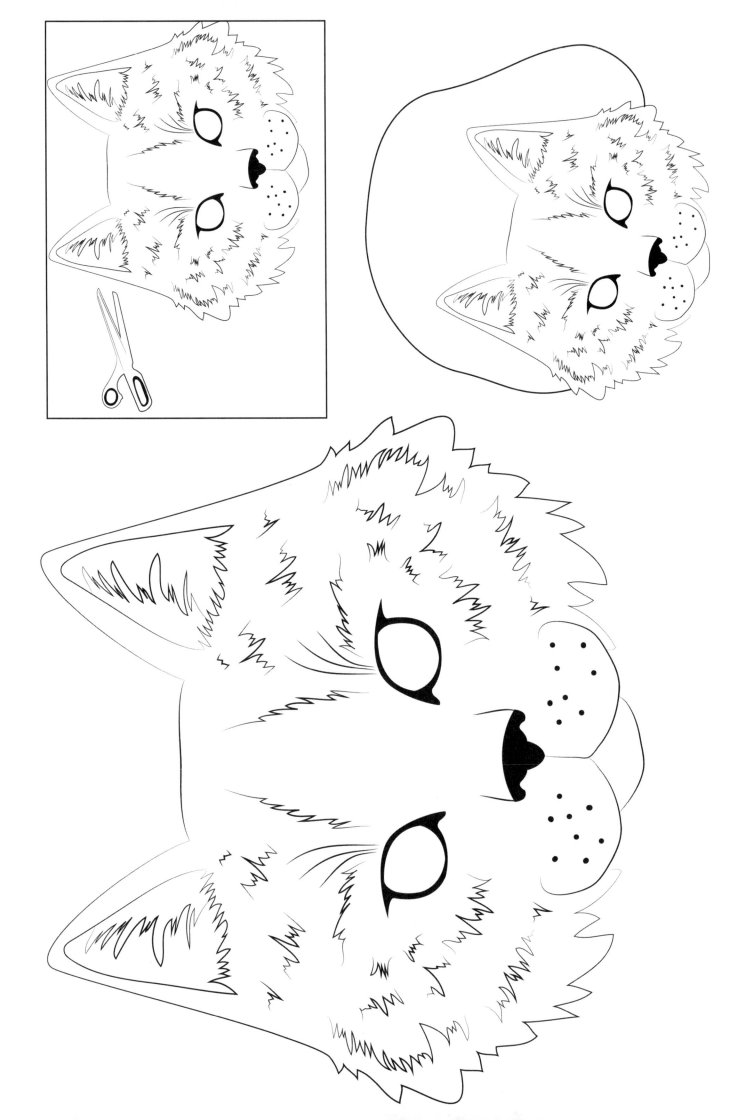

LEAF CROWN

CROWN

1. Colour in and cut out.

2. Staple, glue or use sticky tape to make the circlet.

TIARA

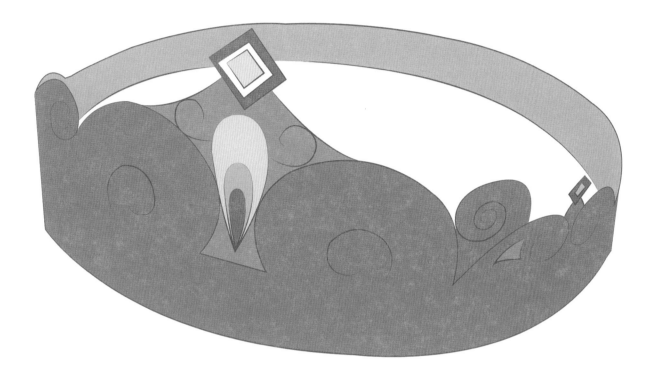

1. Colour in and cut out.

2. Staple, glue or use sticky tape to make the circlet.

Flower crown

MOUSTACHES

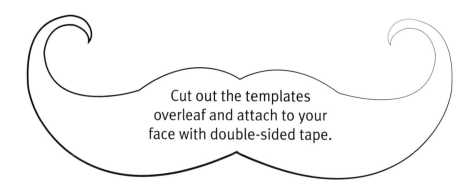

Cut out the templates
overleaf and attach to your
face with double-sided tape.

Witches' claws

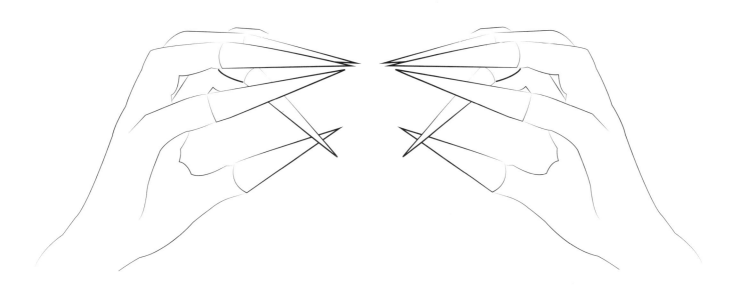

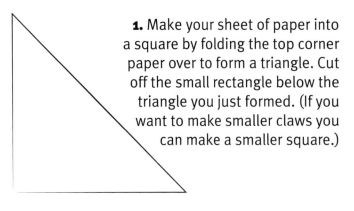

1. Make your sheet of paper into a square by folding the top corner paper over to form a triangle. Cut off the small rectangle below the triangle you just formed. (If you want to make smaller claws you can make a smaller square.)

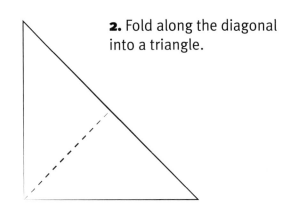

2. Fold along the diagonal into a triangle.

3. Then again along the diagonal into another triangle.

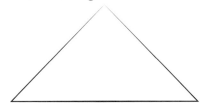

4. Fold the point of the triangle down to the longest edge.

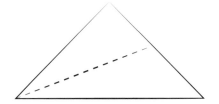

5. Fold in the right-hand point, crease and unfold.

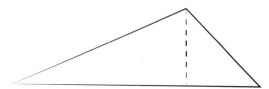

6. Tuck the right-hand point into the pocket.

7. Open up to create a cone shape and slip over your finger.

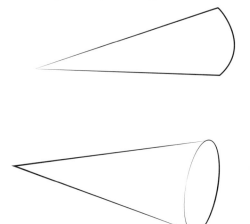

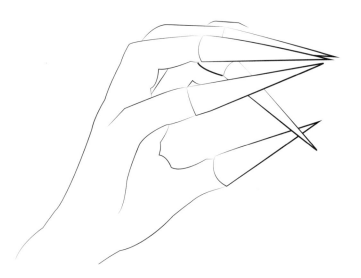

BEARDS

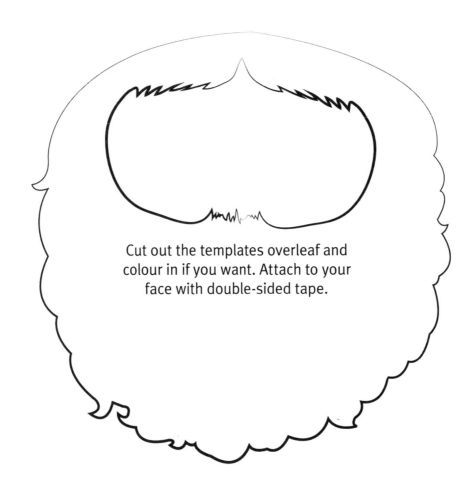

Cut out the templates overleaf and colour in if you want. Attach to your face with double-sided tape.

Necktie

For those occasions you have to attend an unexpected meeting.

BOW TIES

1. Colour in the templates and cut out.

2. Turn over to the reverse, fold one of the bows back and glue in place in the middle. Repeat with the other bow.

3. Wrap the centre of the bow around the middle and glue in place at the back.

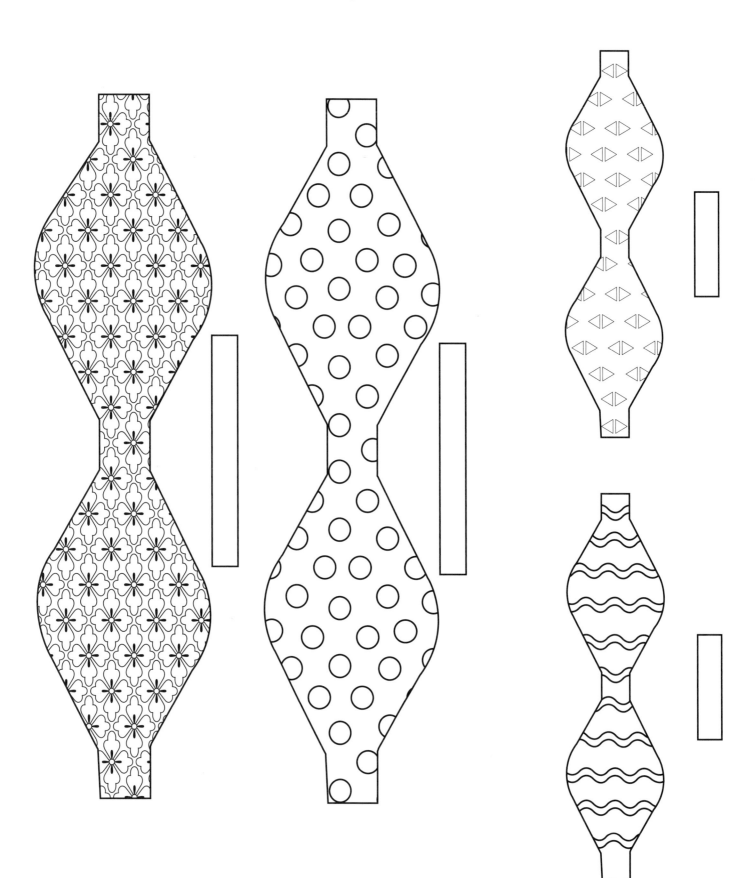

Spectacles

PARTY HAT

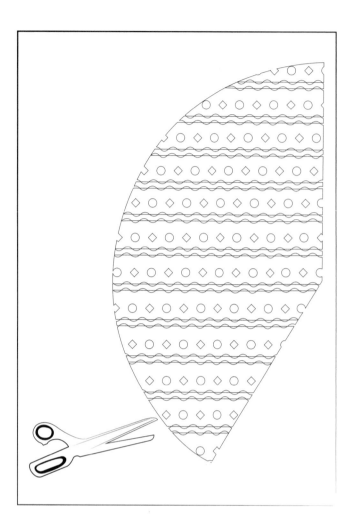

1. Cut out the template. Bring the two ends of the half circle together to form a cone (the more the edges overlap, the smaller the cone). Secure with tape or a staple.

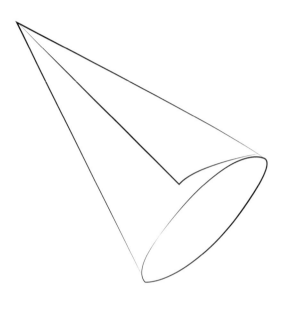

2. Cut a large elastic band in half and knot at both ends.

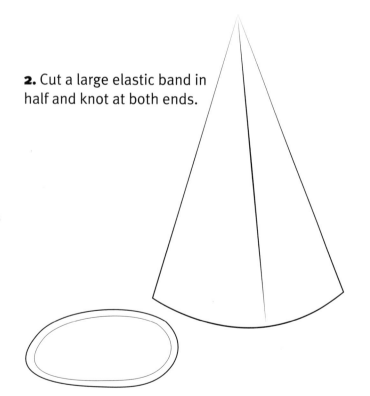

3. Staple the elastic to the inside of the cone.

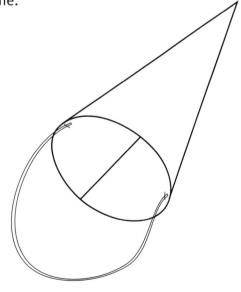

Jester's Hat

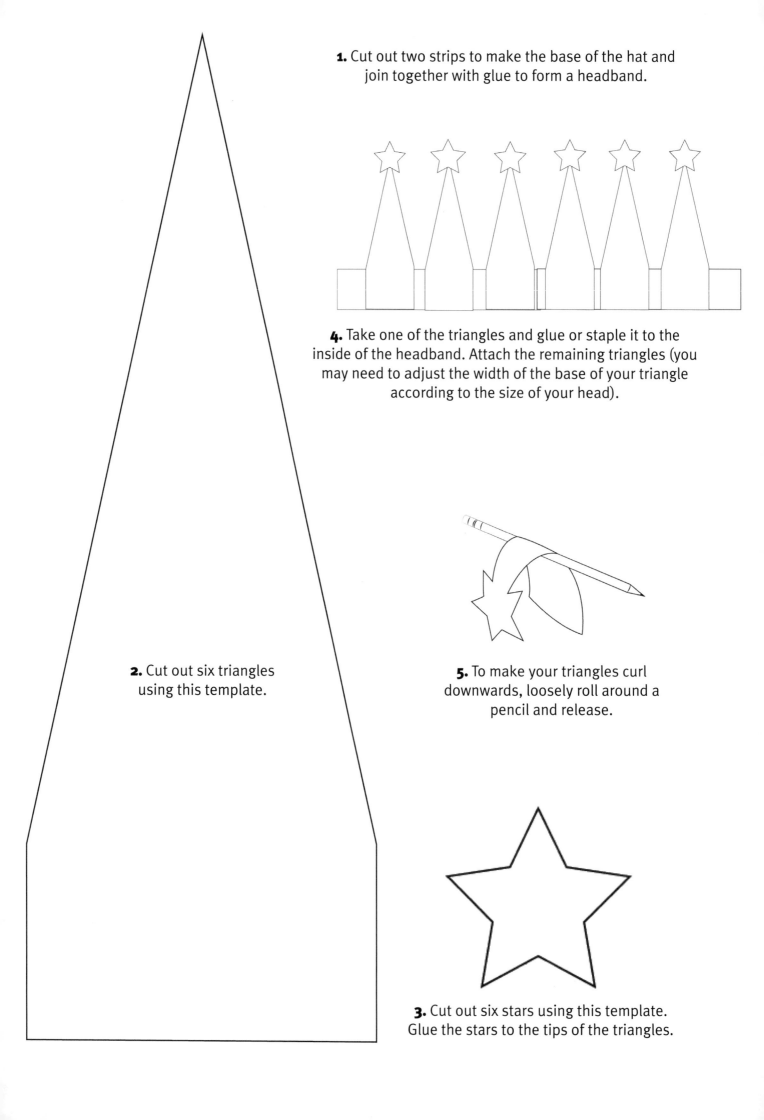

1. Cut out two strips to make the base of the hat and join together with glue to form a headband.

4. Take one of the triangles and glue or staple it to the inside of the headband. Attach the remaining triangles (you may need to adjust the width of the base of your triangle according to the size of your head).

2. Cut out six triangles using this template.

5. To make your triangles curl downwards, loosely roll around a pencil and release.

3. Cut out six stars using this template. Glue the stars to the tips of the triangles.

Paper Visor

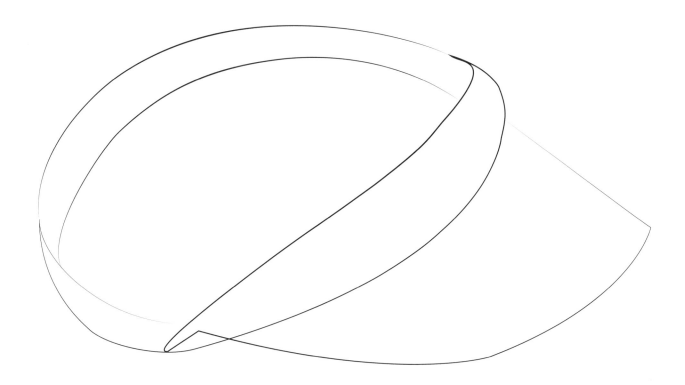

1. Cut out the template overleaf and decorate the visor.

2. Carefully crease along the dotted lines – use a pencil to crease along the curved line.

3. Fold up along the straight dotted line, then fold down the curved dotted line. As you do so, the paper will curve into a visor shape. Glue in place.

4. Cut out the strips of paper to make a band and attach it to the visor with glue.

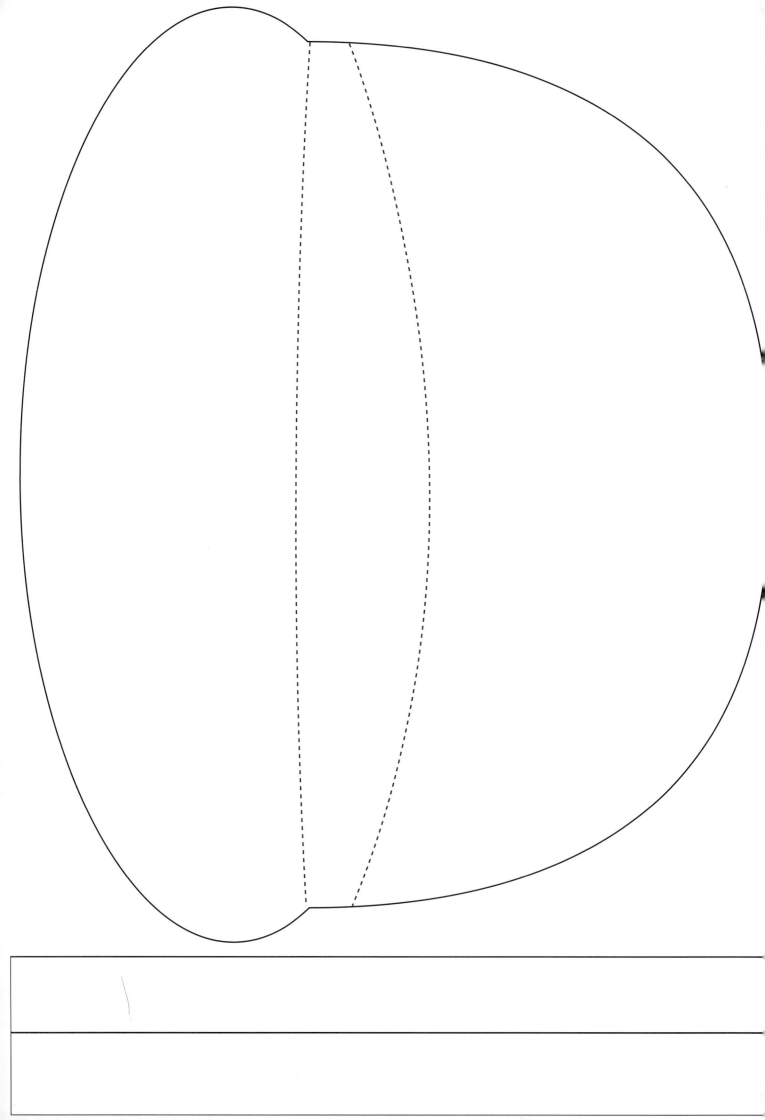

Christmas
headband

EGYPTIAN COLLAR

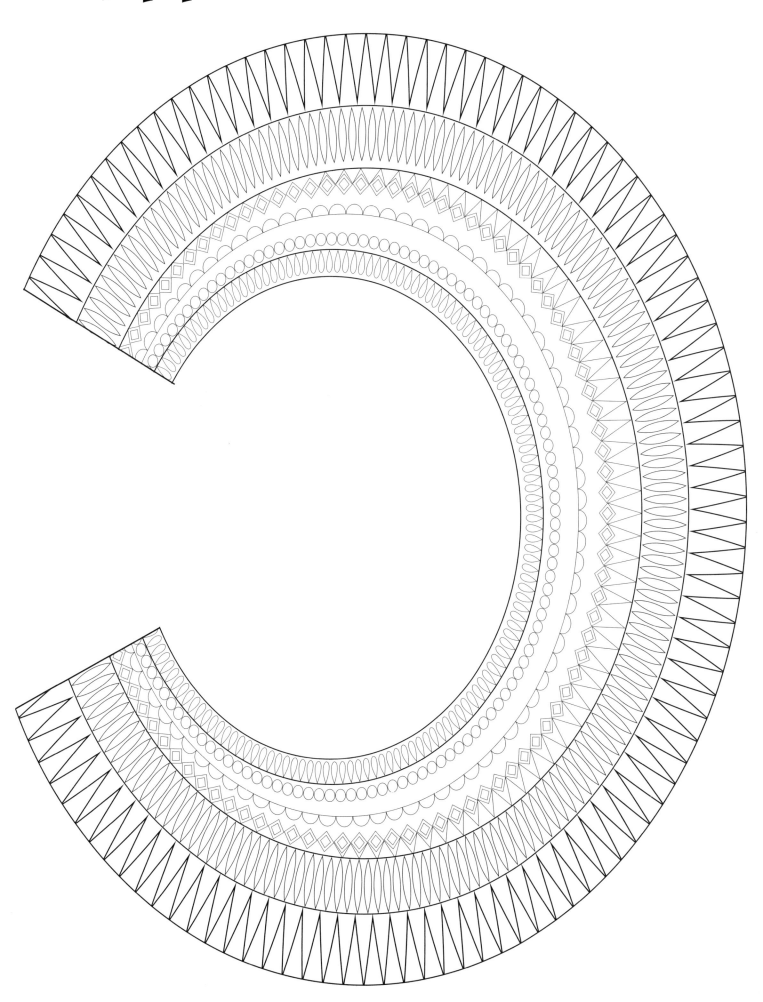

Colour in the template overleaf, then cut out.

Rose corsage

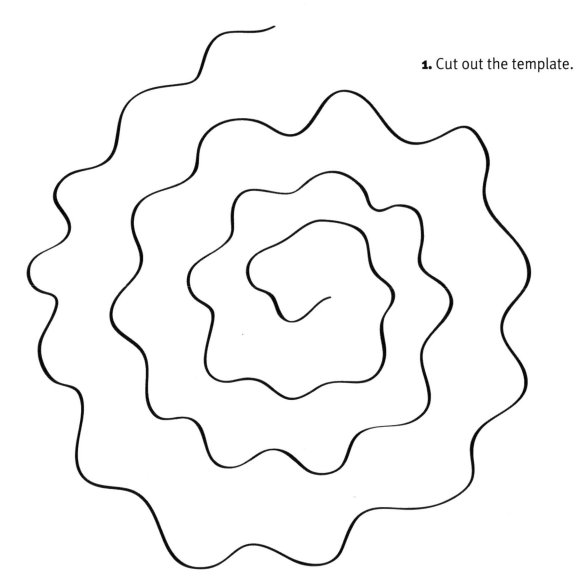

1. Cut out the template.

2. Carefully roll the paper from the end until you reach the middle.

3. Secure the centre with a blob of glue. Once you let go of the rolled flower, it will unroll slightly, giving the flower a looser look.

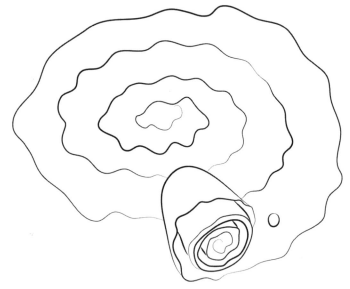

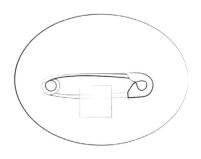

4. If you want your flower to appear more natural, carefully bend the petals open.

5. If you want to wear as a corsage, cut out a base slightly smaller than your flower. Attach a safety pin to the back and glue the flower to the front.

Paper Beads

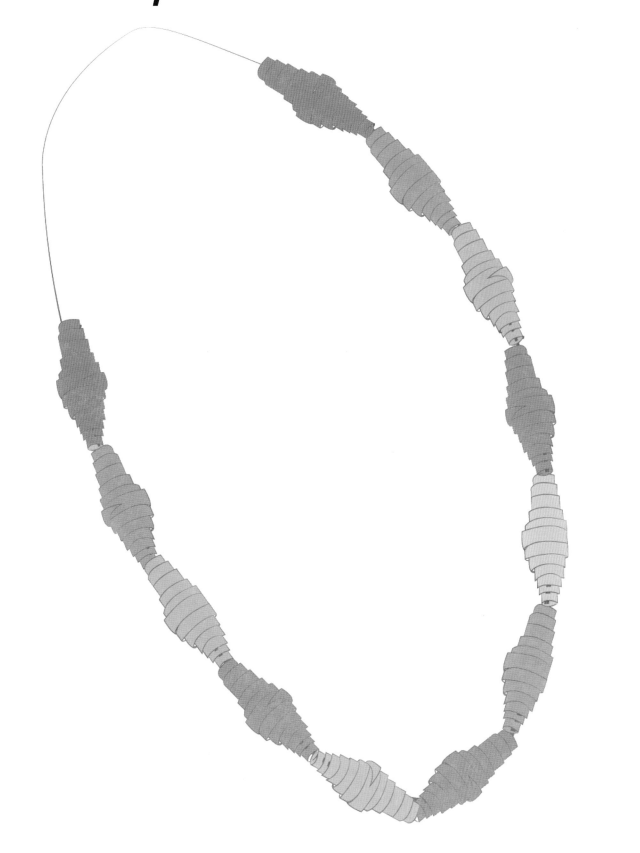

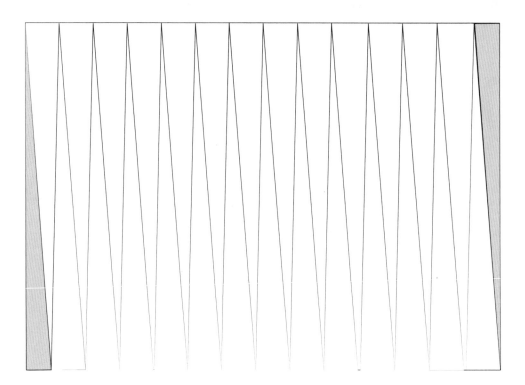

1. Take your sheet of paper and measure 1.5cm in from the top. Then mark off every 3cm. Do the same from the bottom, but just mark 3cm intervals. Join these marks together so you have a series of long thin triangles.

2. Cut out the triangles, discarding the two incomplete shapes at either end.

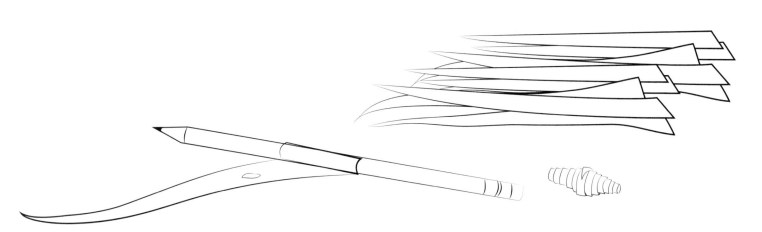

3. Take a pencil and tightly roll one of the triangles around it, starting at the widest end. When you are a centimetre or so along, add a dab of glue, then continue rolling. Keep adding glue at intervals until you get to the last 3cm. Here, add a thin layer of glue to the rest of the paper and complete the roll. Slip your 'bead' off the pencil and put aside to dry whilst you make the rest of your beads.

POP-UP CARD

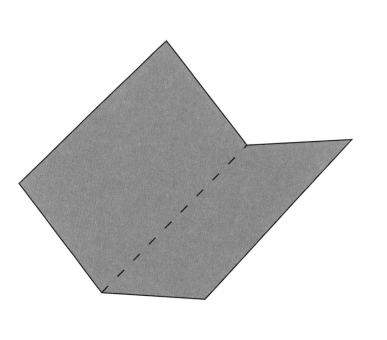
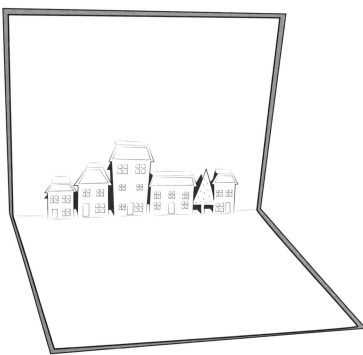

1. On the template overleaf, use a craft knife to cut out the solid lines which outline the houses and tree, including the sides of the tabs above each house.

2. Now carefully fold along the dotted lines so that the houses pop out as shown.

3. Insert into another sheet of folded A4.

Cut-out Valentine card

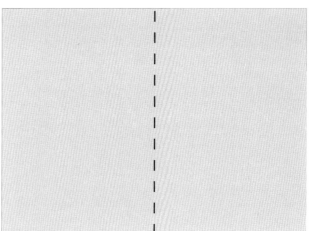

1. Cut out the shaded area overleaf with a craft knife.

2. Score along the dotted line with the reverse side of your craft knife blade.

3. Do the same to the inside paper.

4. Apply a line of glue along the edge of the backfold of the inside paper and stick inside your card.

WOVEN HEART

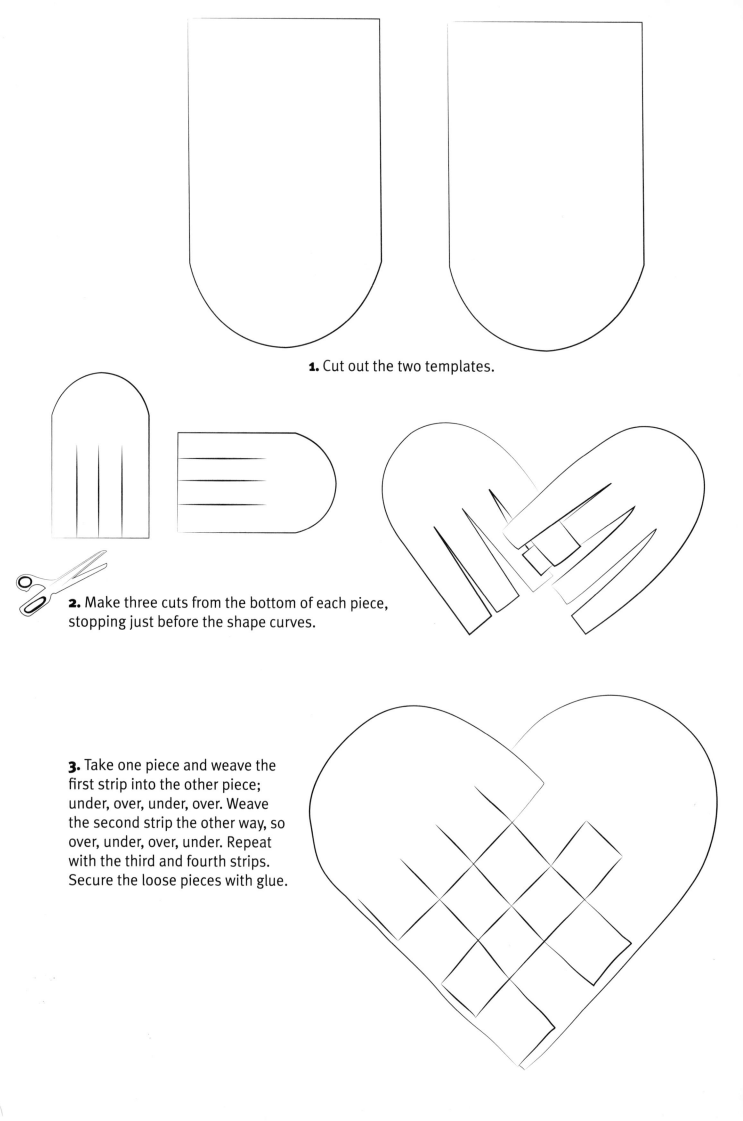

1. Cut out the two templates.

2. Make three cuts from the bottom of each piece, stopping just before the shape curves.

3. Take one piece and weave the first strip into the other piece; under, over, under, over. Weave the second strip the other way, so over, under, over, under. Repeat with the third and fourth strips. Secure the loose pieces with glue.

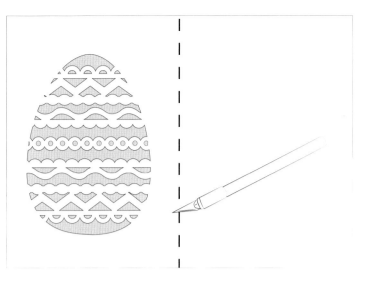

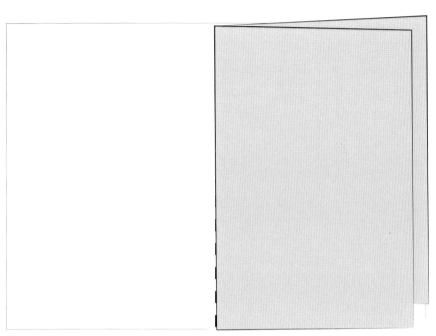

1. Cut out the shaded area on the template overleaf with a craft knife.

2. Score along the dotted line with the reverse side of your craft knife blade.

3. Do the same to the inside paper.

4. Apply a line of glue along the edge of the backfold of the inside paper and stick inside your card.

Cut-out Easter card

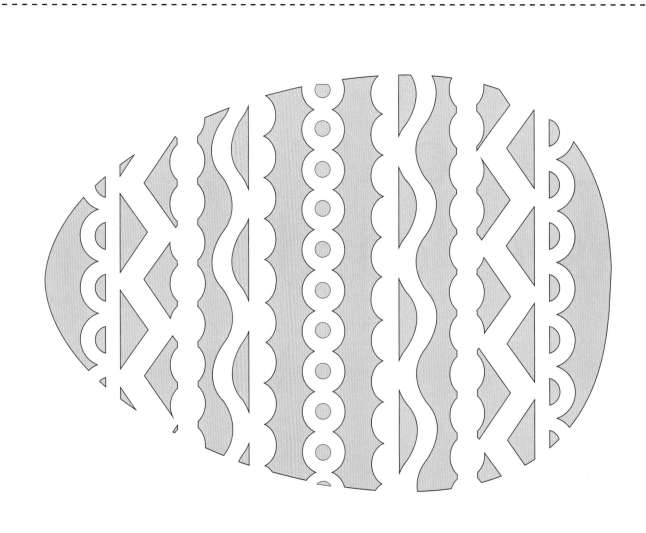

Children's Birthday Card

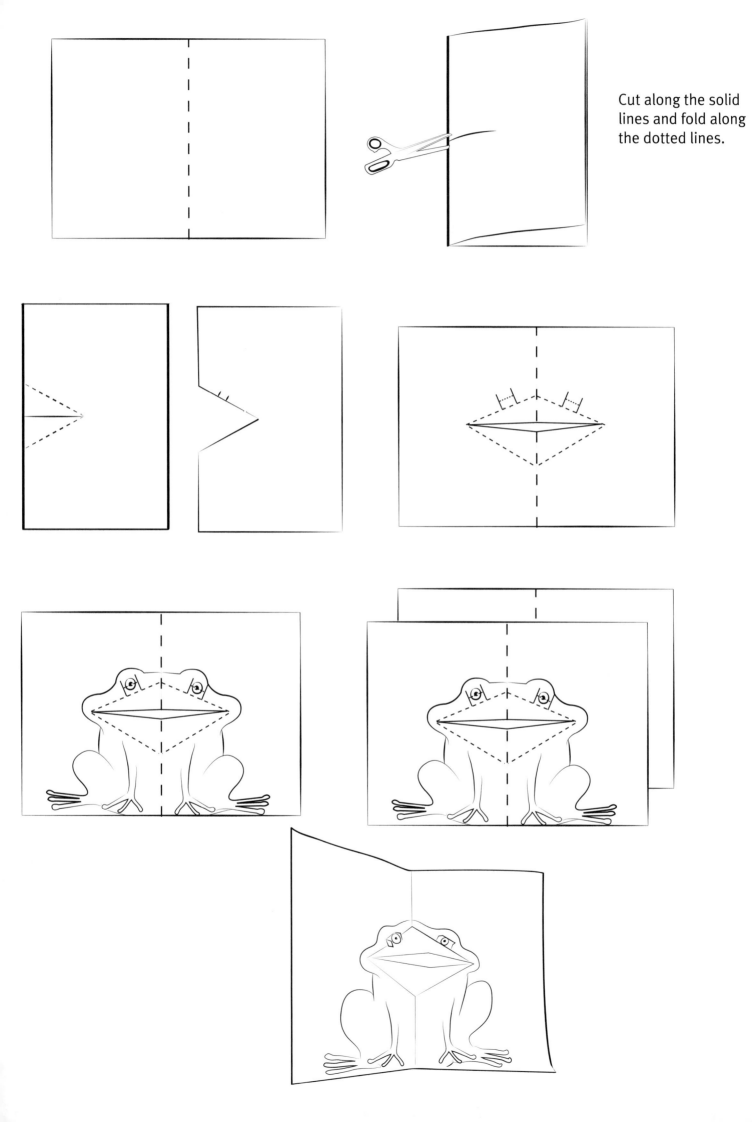

Cut along the solid lines and fold along the dotted lines.

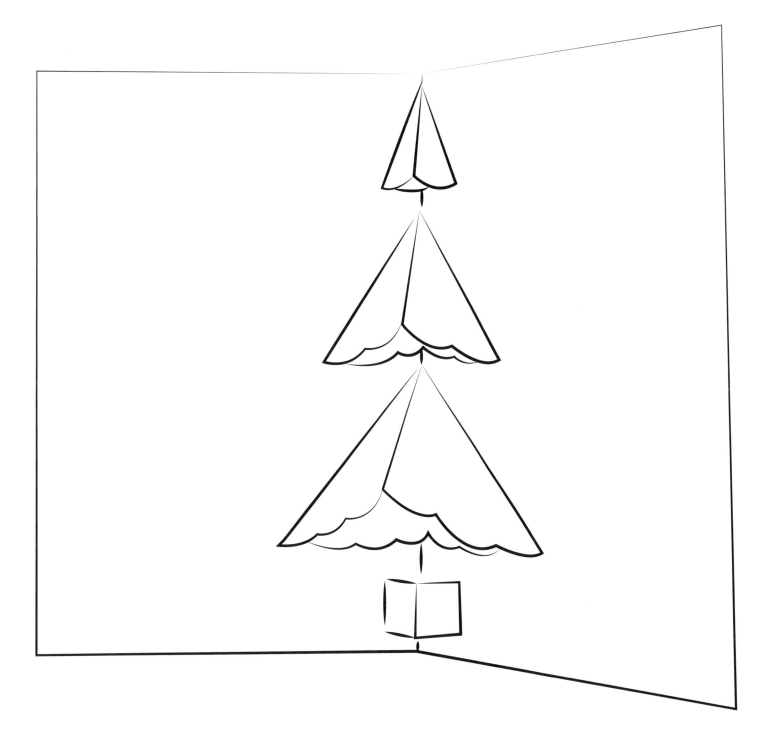

Christmas Card

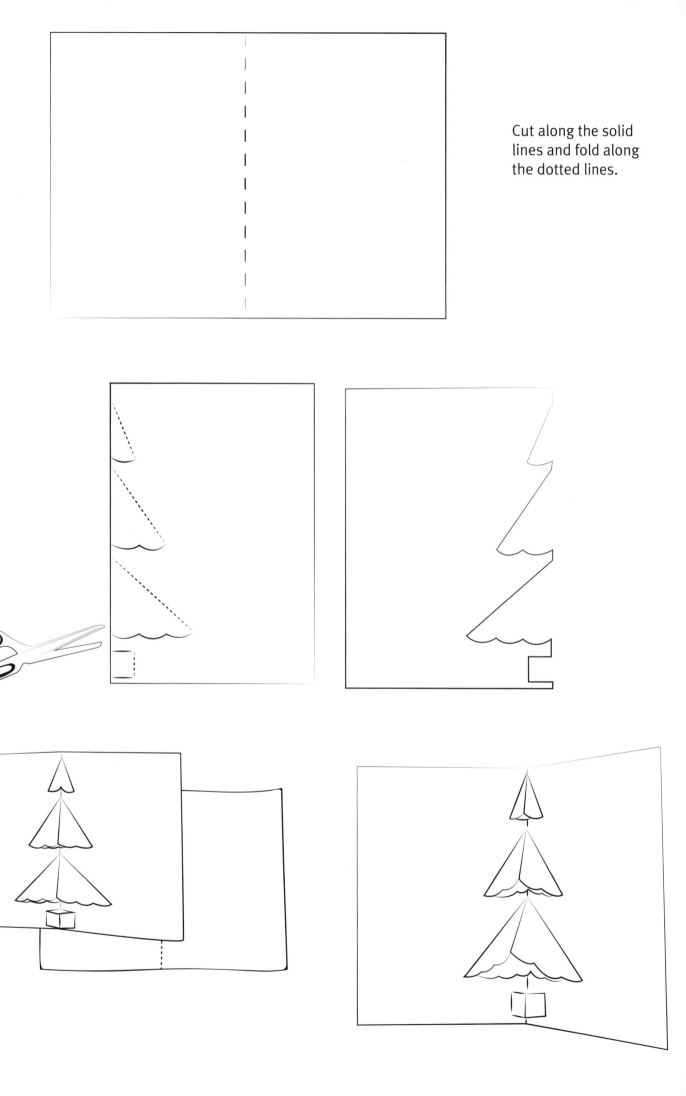

Cut along the solid lines and fold along the dotted lines.

Christmas Tags

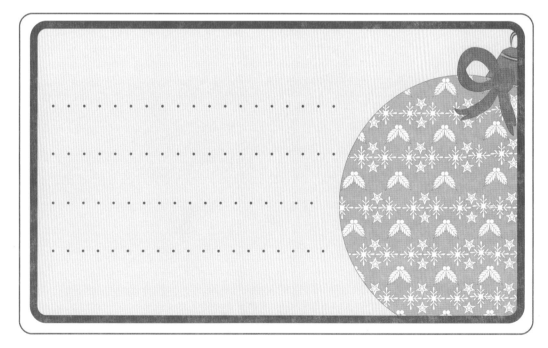

1. Colour in the tags overleaf.

2. Write in your message.

3. Stick on your present.

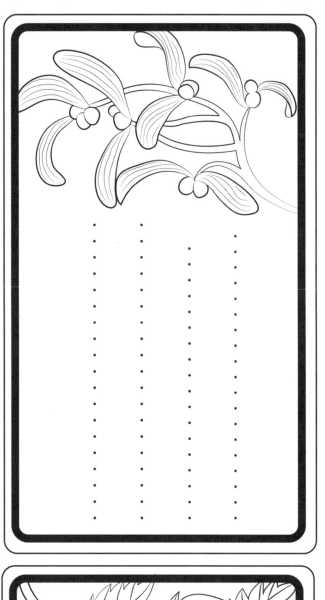

Gift bag

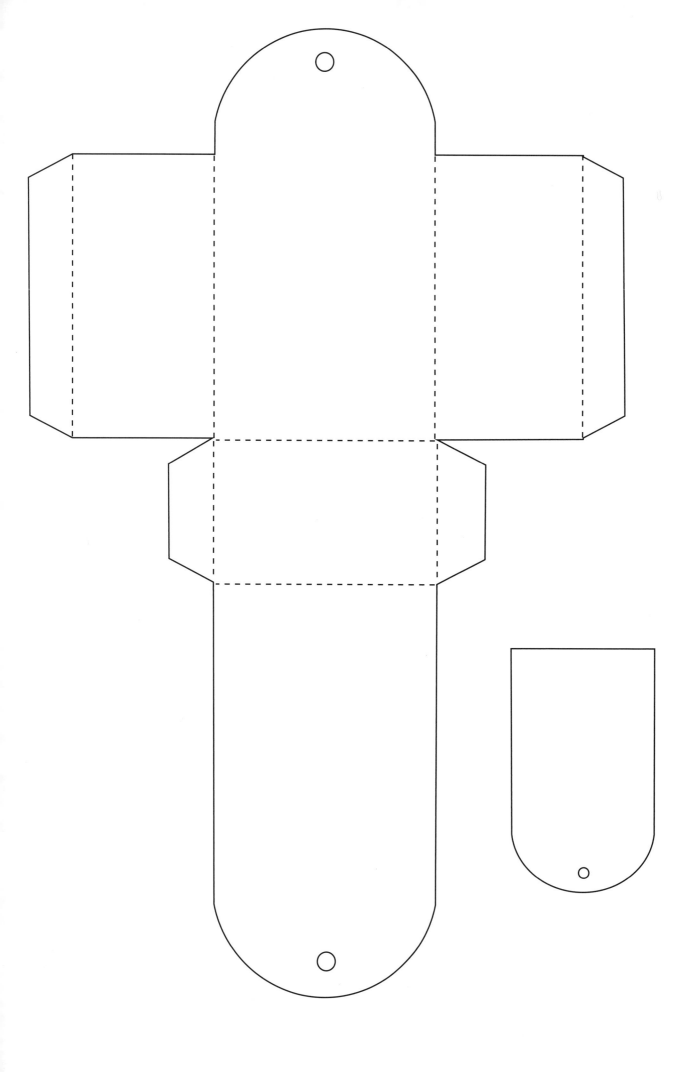

Decorated letter

MONEY ENVELOPE

1. Colour in the design, then cut out.

2. Fold along all four inside lines, then unfold the top and left (large) flap.

3. Apply glue to the right and bottom flaps.

4. Fold over the large flap.
The top flap is the envelope's open end, which can be tucked into place.

ENVELOPE

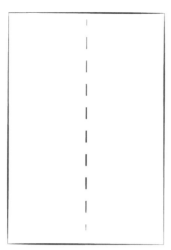 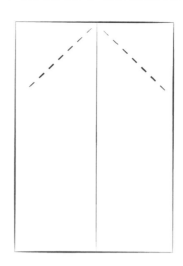

1. Fold the paper in half lengthways. Unfold it so that you have a crease in the middle.

2. Fold the top right corner to the centre crease.

3. Fold the top left corner in the same way.

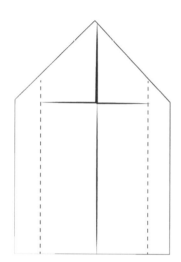 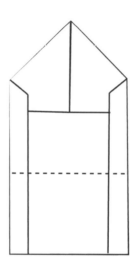  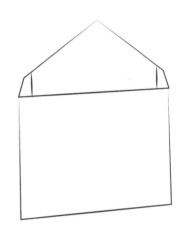 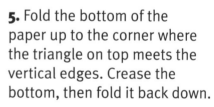

4. Take the left edge of the paper, beneath the triangle, and fold the right edge towards the centre by about half of the triangle's width. Repeat with the right edge of the paper.

5. Fold the bottom of the paper up to the corner where the triangle on top meets the vertical edges. Crease the bottom, then fold it back down.

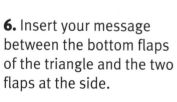 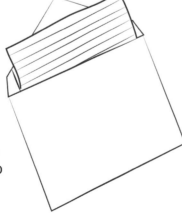 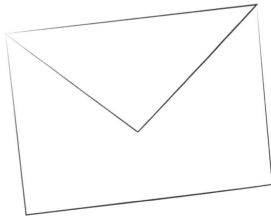

6. Insert your message between the bottom flaps of the triangle and the two flaps at the side.

7. Close the envelope using a small piece of tape to attach the flap to the back of the envelope. For extra security, use tape to close the sides.

Send a
secret message

1. Dip a cotton bud into milk and write your message.

2. Allow to dry.

3. To read the message, the paper will need to be
exposed to heat – a light bulb will do.
The milk will heat up at a slower rate than the paper,
which will cause your message to reappear.